SO-CEZ-070

Essential
Venice

AAA Publishing 1000 AAA Drive, Heathrow, Florida 32746

Venice: Regions and Best places to see

 Best places to see 34–55

 Featured sight

Original text by Teresa Fisher

Revised and updated by Sally Roy

Edited, designed and produced by AA Publishing
© AA Media Limited 2010
Maps © AA Media Limited 2010

ISBN 978-1-59508-382-1

Published in the United States by AAA Publishing,
1000 AAA Drive, Heathrow, Florida 32746
Published in the United Kingdom by AA Publishing

Color separation: MRM Graphics Ltd
Printed and bound in Italy by Printer Trento S.r.l.

A04015
Maps in this title produced from:
map data © New Holland Publishing (South Africa) (PTY) Limited 2009
mapping © ISTITUTO GEOGRAFICO DE AGOSTINI S.p.A., NOVARA 2009
Transport map © Communicarta Ltd, UK

About this book

Symbols are used to denote the following categories:

- ✚ map reference to maps on cover
- ✉ address or location
- ☎ telephone number
- ◷ opening times
- ✋ admission charge
- ❚❚ restaurant or café on premises or nearby
- Ⓜ nearest underground train station
- 🚌 nearest bus/tram route
- 🚆 nearest overground train station
- ⛴ nearest ferry stop
- ✈ nearest airport
- ❓ other practical information
- ❶ tourist information office
- ► indicates the page where you will find a fuller description

This book is divided into six sections.

The essence of Venice pages 6–19
Introduction; Features; Food and Drink; Short Break including the 10 Essentials

Planning pages 20–33
Before You Go; Getting There; Getting Around; Being There

Best places to see pages 34–55
The unmissable highlights of any visit to Venice

Best things to do pages 56–75
Stunning views; speciality shops; places to take the children and more

Exploring pages 76–171
The best places to visit in Venice, organized by area

Excursions pages 172–183
Places to visit out of town

Maps
All map references are to the maps on the covers. For example, Palazzo Ducale has the reference ✚ 21J – indicating the grid square in which it is to be found

Prices
An indication of the cost of restaurants at attractions is given by € signs: €€€ denotes higher prices, €€ denotes average prices, € denotes lower prices

Hotel prices
Prices for a double room per night:
€ budget (under €120); €€ moderate (€120–€220); €€€ expensive (€220–€300); €€€€ luxury (over €300)

Restaurant prices
Price for a three-course meal per person without drinks: € budget (under €30); €€ moderate (€30–€55); €€€ expensive (over €55)

Contents

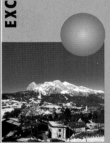

The essence of...

THE ESSENCE OF VENICE

Venice is a city that charms and captivates, the historic flagship of a mighty fleet of islands in the lagoon. To discover its true character you should first see the main sights – the Grand Canal, St Mark's Square, the Doges' Palace. But then take time to explore the picture-postcard backwaters with their hidden squares and tiny churches. There's a secret side to Venice too, only accessible by water. Once afloat, you enter a different world, seeing the city as it was designed to be seen – through snatched glimpses into ancient houses, secluded gardens and boatyards with gondolas waiting for repair. This is where the real essence of Venice lies.

features

One of the most painted, filmed and written about cities in the world, Venice is incredibly beautiful; nothing quite prepares you for that first glimpse of distant domes and spires emerging from the flat, grey waters like a mirage. Or on a sunny day when the water sparkles like a thousand tiny lanterns, its magic is breathtaking. Within the city, murky canal water laps the bases of dreamlike buildings, creating a slightly disorienting, rocking effect enhanced by the gentle rattle of the wind as it brushes against the boats and mooring poles. Behind the canals lie tiny, winding alleys in which even an expert map reader soon gets lost and all sense of urgency has to be forgotten. Time is irrelevant; this place weaves its spell and lingers in the memory until the next visit releases another onslaught on the senses.

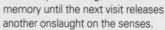

THE CITY

- Height above sea level: 80cm (31in)
- Height of 1966 floods: 2m (6ft)
- Highest point: Campanile at 99m (325ft)
- Size of city (from east to west): 5km (3 miles)
- Size of city (from north to south): 2km (1 mile)
- Size eqivalent to: Central Park, New York

- Number of districts *(sestieri)*: 6
- Number of canals: 177
- Number of bridges (estimated): 400
- Number of alleys (estimated): 3,000
- Number of churches (estimated): 200
- Rate of sinking (annual): 0cm (no longer sinking)
- Buildings on Grand Canal with damaged foundations: 60 per cent
- Visitors per year (estimated): between 13 and 14 million

POPULATION
- Population in heyday of Venetian Republic (estimated): 200,000
- Population in 1950 (estimated): 140,000
- Population in 2008 (estimated): 60,000
- People leaving Venice annually (estimated): 1,500

ECONOMIC FACTORS
- Cost of living: 1.5 per cent higher than Milan, 4 per cent higher than Rome
- Percentage of workforce involved in tourism: over 50 per cent
- Number of gift shops (estimated): 500
- Number of plumbers (estimated): 10

THE LAGOON
- Length: 56km (30 miles)
- Width: 8–14km (5–9 miles)
- Surface area: 550sq km (212sq miles)

food & drink

Its reputation for dull, unimaginative cooking, high prices and surly service is not fair to Venice. It is true that restaurants tend to be more expensive – beware hidden costs – than those on the mainland since almost everything but some of the fish has to be imported by barge, and along the tourist trails the waiters can become as jaded as their customers, particularly in summer. That said, you can eat well in Venice.

ORIGINS OF VENETIAN CUISINE

Venice sits at the crossroads of the former trading routes linking Europe to the East. For centuries there was the desire for the spices of the Orient, and men plying those goods would often rest up in the city, leaving their influence. Exotic foods from Arabia, Turkey and Asia found their way into the local cuisine. The use of spices in the rice dishes, the addition of spiced vinegar and nuts and raisins to the sardines, and foods preserved for the sailors on the long sea journeys all contributed to a unique diet. Venetian chefs

utilized the local fresh produce – vegetables, fruit, and river and sea fish – combining them with the foreign imports to produce great banquets and lavish hospitality for which the city was renowned. Tastes may have simplified over the years, but the Venetian cuisine still retains something of its earlier origins.

FINDING THE REAL THING

Local people won't accept the mediocre food that is often offered in a city so dominated by tourists, so you need to search out the traditional restaurants frequented by Venetians. You only have to look in the Rialto markets to see what is available. Two of the most familiar Venetian main dishes are acquired tastes: *fegato alla Veneziana* (sliced calves' liver with onion) and *seppie* (squid) cooked in its own

black ink with *polenta* (cornmeal cake). Venetians are good at creating delectable sweets, particularly the light and creamy *tiramisù*, a delicious cold confection of chocolate, coffee, mascarpone cheese and brandy. Another way to get a taste of Italian food is to try some of the many local snacks known as *cicheti*, usually displayed on counters and not dissimilar to Spanish tapas. These include garlicky *polpette* (meatballs), *pizzete* (mini-pizzas),

various types of seafood and slices of fried vegetables. Take a look at the selection in the windows of the old-fashioned Venetian bakeries and patisseries to see how the traditional pastries have survived. They may not always suit your palate but are worth a try. Two classic biscuits are interesting – *baicoli* and *busolai*. The first is a light, dry biscuit, its shape resembling a fish, which is best eaten with a drink or ice cream. The latter,

the *busolai*, comes from the island of Burano and is seriously sweet with a hint of aniseed. For a daintier and more refined treat try some of the more sophisticated shops or cafés where you will also find the *brioscia*, the ubiquitous breakfast ingredient, the melt-in-the-mouth croissant.

EATING OUT

Those enjoying the higher trattoria style of cooking will not be disappointed. Venetian restaurants offer the same range of basic Italian dishes as will be found throughout the country, but their local specialities are more simple than say Florence, Bologna or Rome. For a first course try *zuppa di pesce* (fish soup), which is so

full of shellfish, shrimp and white fish that it is best followed by something light, or try *prosciutto crudo* (Parma ham) with fresh figs. Fish and seafood are expensive but popular with a plentiful supply of fish coming from the Adriatic – try the *antipasto di frutti di mare*, a particular favourite. You'll find some unusual seafood too – *granseola* (spider crab), *capelonghe* (razor shells) and *schie* (miniature prawns).

AND TO DRINK

When ordering drinks, *una ombra* (which means 'shade') will produce a glass of white house wine, unless you request *rosso* (red). Ombra comes from the old tradition of drinking wine in the shade of the piazza. Head for a *bàcaro* (a traditional wine bar), for a glass or two. A *spritz* is a popular drink in Venice (a glass of white wine served with an apertif such as Campari) – watch out, they can be strong!

THE ESSENCE OF VENICE

If you only have a short time to visit Venice and would like to take home some unforgettable memories, you can do something local and capture the real flavour of the city. The following suggestions will give you a wide range of sights and experiences that won't take long, won't cost very much and will make your visit a very special one.

● **Take a boat** on the Grand Canal (➤ 72–73) by day to marvel at its majestic water-lapped palaces and gaily painted mooring poles or by night to catch glimpses of the grand illuminated interiors.

● **Visit the Rialto markets** (➤ 130–131) at the crack of dawn before the crowds arrive.

● **A mid-morning coffee** in Europe's finest square, atmospheric Piazza San Marco (➤ 44–45), will both delight and bankrupt you.

- **Stroll along the southern shore** of the Dorsoduro (➤ 141–153), with its boathouses, bars and cafés. Go at dusk, when Venetians take their *passeggiata* (evening stroll).

- **Indulge yourself** in the romance of a gondola ride (➤ 27) at sunset and capture the true magic of Venice.

THE ESSENCE OF VENICE

● **Take the elevator** up to the top of the
Campanile (► 80–81) or San Giorgio Maggiore
(► 46–47) for breathtaking views.

● **Indulge in some window shopping** –
Venetian specialities include beads, masks, paper
products, textiles and food.

● **Get lost in the labyrinthine alleys** and
backwaters of the city, or visit the outlying
islands (► 159–171) for a taste of Venetian life
off the main tourist drag.

● **See Venice by night.**
The canals have a magical beauty and many of the main monuments are floodlit after dark.

● **End your day Venetian-style** with an ice cream or a *digestif* (liqueur) in one of the city's countless café-ringed squares. One of the best ice-cream shops is Paolin (➤ 95).

Planning

Before you go

WHEN TO GO

	JAN	FEB	MAR	APR	MAY	JUN	JUL	AUG	SEP	OCT	NOV	DEC
	6°C	8°C	12°C	15°C	20°C	23°C	26°C	25°C	21°C	16°C	12°C	7°C
	43°F	46°F	54°F	59°F	68°F	73°F	79°F	77°F	70°F	61°F	54°F	45°F

⬤ High season ⬤ Low season

The best times to visit Venice are March to early June and mid-September to the end of October, when the weather is generally fine but not too hot. Avoid July and August, when the city is not only hot and humid but also often extremely crowded. Winters can be very cold and damp, with chill easterly winds and mists off the lagoon. Late winter can bring crystal clear, cold and sunny days. Snow is uncommon, but always possible. However, bear in mind that this is a city that is beautiful, and has plenty to offer, whatever the weather, but can be busy year-round. Particularly crowded times are during Carnevale (usually around 10 days in February), Easter, Christmas, New Year and during school holidays.

WHAT YOU NEED

● Required   Some countries require a passport to
○ Suggested   remain valid for a minimum period (usually
▲ Not required   at least six months) beyond the date of
                entry – check before you travel.

	UK	Germany	USA	Netherlands	Spain
Passport (or National Identity Card where applicable)	●	●	●	●	●
Visa (regulations can change – check before you travel)	▲	▲	▲	▲	▲
Onward or Return Ticket	▲	▲	▲	▲	▲
Health Inoculations (tetanus and polio)	▲	▲	▲	▲	▲
Health Documentation (▶ 23, Health Insurance)	●	●	●	●	●
Travel Insurance	○	○	○	○	○
Driving Licence (national)	●	●	●	●	●
Car Insurance Certificate	●	●	●	●	●
Car Registration Document	●	●	●	●	●

WEBSITES

www.hellovenezia.com
www.museicivicivenezia.it
www.chorusvenezia.org
Tourist Authority:
www.turismovenezia.it

City Council:
www.comune.venezia.it
Italian State Tourist Office:
www.enit.it
Transport Authority: www.actv.it

TOURIST OFFICES AT HOME

In the UK
Italian State Tourist Office (ENIT)
1 Princes Street
London W1B 2AY
☎ 020 7408 1254
www.enit.it;
www.italiantourism.com

In the US
Italian State Tourist Office (ENIT)
630 Fifth Avenue
Suite 1565
Rockefeller Center
New York, NY 10111
☎ 212/245-5618

HEALTH INSURANCE

Nationals of EU and certain other countries can get reduced-cost emergency healthcare in Italy with the relevant documentation – an EHIC (European Health Insurance Card), although private medical insurance is still advised and is essential for all other visitors.

Dental treatment is expensive in Italy but should be covered by private medical insurance. A list of dentists *(dentisti)* can be found in the yellow pages of the telephone directory or online at www.paginegialle.it

TIME DIFFERENCES

GMT	Venice	Germany	USA (NY)	Netherlands	Spain
12 noon	1PM	1PM	7AM	1PM	1PM

Venice is one hour ahead of Greenwich Mean Time (GMT +1), but from late March, when clocks are put forward one hour, until late October, Italian summer time (GMT +2) operates.

NATIONAL HOLIDAYS

1 Jan *New Year's Day*
6 Jan *Epiphany*
Mar/Apr *Easter Monday*
25 Apr *Liberation Day and patron saint's day (San Marco)*

1 May *Labour Day*
29 Jun *St. Peter and St Paul*
15 Aug *Assumption of the Virgin*
1 Nov *All Saints' Day*

8 Dec *Feast of the Immaculate Conception*
25 Dec *Christmas Day*
26 Dec *Santo Stefano*

WHAT'S ON WHEN

January *Regata della Befana* (6 Jan): The first of more than 100 regattas to be held on the lagoon throughout the year is on Epiphany.

February *Carnevale* (10 days before Lent): The carnival was abolished by the French in 1797 but revived in 1979 with great success. At first largely a Venetian festival, it is now international and, some complain, over-elaborate. Masks and fancy dress – which can be bought or rented in the city – are worn all day and most of the night. A daily schedule of events includes dancing at night in a *campo*, where mulled wine and traditional sugared cakes are sold from stands.

April *Festa di San Marco* (25 Apr): The feast day of St Mark, Venice's patron saint. A gondola race from Sant'Elena to the Punta della Dogana marks the day and men give women a red rose.

May *Festa della Sensa* (Sunday after Ascencion Day): The Mayor of Venice re-enacts the ceremony of the Marriage of Venice with the Sea. In the old days, the Doge would be rowed out to sea in his ceremonial barge to cast a gold wedding ring into the Adriatic, but the occasion is now only a faint echo of the original.
Vogalonga (Sunday following *La Sensa*): A 32km (20-mile) rowing race in which anyone can join in any type of oared boat from San Marco to Burano and back.

June *Biennale* (Jun–Sep; alternates annually between visual arts and architecture, with architecture in even-numbered years): International arts festival.
Festa di San Pietro (last weekend in Jun): Celebrates the feast of St Peter; centred on his church in Castello, it's a lively event with concerts, dancing and food stands.

July *Festa del Redentore* (third weekend in Jul): This event involves the building of a bridge of boats across the Giudecca Canal to the church of the Redentore and was begun as a festival in thanksgiving for the ending of a plague more than four centuries ago. People come out to picnic and fireworks mark the occasion.

August/September *Mostra del Cinema Venezia* (12 days from last week in Aug): The high-profile international Venice Film Festival is held on the Lido; it's Italy's version of Cannes.

September *Regata Storica* (first Sunday in Sep): The most spectacular event of the Venetian year, which involves gondola races and an entertaining procession up the Grand Canal of boats and barges manned by Venetians in historic costume.

November *Festa della Salute* (21 Nov): A procession makes its way across the Grand Canal on floating bridges to the church of the Salute to give thanks for the ending of another plague of 1630.

December *La Befana* (Christmas, New Year): Celebrations for the festive season.

Getting there

BY AIR

Marco Polo Airport

13km (8 miles) to city centre

🚌	N/A
🚐	25 minutes
🚕	15 minutes

Treviso Airport Airport

30km (19 miles) to city centre

🚌	N/A
🚐	45 minutes
🚕	35 minutes

There are direct flights to Venice from all over the world. Scheduled flights arrive at Venice's Marco Polo airport, while the city's second airport, Treviso, caters mostly for charter and some no-frills airlines.

BY RAIL

International and national rail services arrive at Venice's main railway station, Venezia Santa Lucia (Venezia SL), at the western end of the Grand Canal. Boats leave from outside the station. Some rail services stop at Venezia Mestre, on the mainland, and do not cross the causeway to Venice.

BY CAR

The A4 autostrada (motorway) provides the most direct car approach to Venice. Leave your vehicle either at the multi-storey garages across the causeway at Piazzale Roma (Autorimessa Comunale, tel 041 272 7301, www.asmvenezia.it), on the island of Tronchetto (Venezia Tronchetto Parking tel 041 520 7555, www.veniceparking.it) or at mainland Fusina (Park Terminal Fusina, tel 041 547 0160, www.terminalfusina.it). All car parks can be booked online and are connected to Venice by *vaporetto*.

BY SEA

Ferries run to Venice from ports across the Adriatic in Croatia, Slovenia and elsewhere. Many cruise liners also dock in the city.

Getting around

PUBLIC TRANSPORT

Vaporetto The *vaporetto*, or water bus, is operated by the public transport system, ACTV; www.actv.it. The main routes run every 10 to 20 minutes during the day. Services are reduced in the evening, especially after midnight. A night service (N) runs along the Grand Canal to the Giudecca and Murano. You can buy a ticket for each journey (€6.50 or €2 for one stop on the Grand Canal) at a ticket office on the pier (if there is one) or pay more for a ticket on board, but if you intend to make several journeys in a day, buy a *biglietto giornaliero* (24-hour ticket; €16) or a *biglietto ore* (72-hour; €33). All tickets must be date-stamped by the automatic machine on the pier before boarding. If you are staying a week, you can buy a weekly *abbonamento* (€50) from ticket offices.

Gondola A gondola is the most enjoyable means of transport in the city, but also the most expensive – around €80 for a four-person gondola. Fares are governed by a tariff for a 40-minute trip, with a surcharge for night trips after 8pm, but, as gondoliers are notorious for overcharging, it is often easiest to establish terms by ordering a gondola via your tour representative or hotel staff. For a memorable outing, take a two-hour gondola ride down the Grand Canal with a picnic supper on board (note that the side canals are usually much calmer). Or take a cruise operated during the summer months by flotillas of gondolas packed with tourists and entertained by singers – providing an ideal opportunity to explore the waterways at an affordable price.

Traghetto Ferry gondolas – *traghetti* – cross the Grand Canal between special piers at seven different points, providing a vital service for pedestrians. They are indicated by a yellow street sign, illustrated with a tiny gondola symbol. The very reasonable fare (as little as €0.50) is paid to the gondolier when you board.

WATER TAXI

Water taxis can be rented from water taxi stands, including ones at the airport and Piazza San Marco. They can also be ordered by telephone (☎ 041 522 2303; www.motoscafivenezia.it). Fares are very expensive, but are regulated by a tariff.

DRIVING

- Italians drive on the right.
- Seat belts must be worn in front seats at all times and in rear seats where fitted.

- Random breath-testing takes place. Never drive under the influence of alcohol.
- Fuel *(benzina)* is more expensive than in the US and most European countries. Filling stations all sell unleaded fuel *(senza piombo)*, but do not always accept credit cards. They are generally open Monday to Saturday 7–12:30, 3–7:30. Motorway service stations open 24 hours.
- In the event of a breakdown call the Automobile Club d'Italia (☎ 116), giving your location, registration number and type of car, and the nearest ACI office will tow you to the nearest ACI garage. This service is free to foreign vehicles, but you will need to produce your car documentation and passport.
- Speed limits are as follows:
  On motorways *(autostrade)* 130kph (80mph)
  On main roads: 110kph (68mph)
  On secondary roads: 90kph (56mph)
  In towns: 50kph (31mph)

CAR RENTAL

The leading international car rental companies have offices at Marco Polo airport. Book a car in advance (essential in peak season) either direct or through a travel agent. Bear in mind that driving in the centre of Venice itself is not possible.

FARES AND CONCESSIONS

Students Visitors between the ages of 14 and 29 can use the Rolling Venice programme, which offers concessions on transportation, museum entry, hotels and restaurants. The pass costs €4 and is obtainable from VeLa and APT offices on production of your passport and two photos . The Venice Card offers similar concessions for all ages and can be purchased at VeLa, ACTV ticket offices and APT tourist offices. The main youth hostel for Venice is Ostello Venezia, Fondamenta della Zitelle, on Guidecca (☎ 041 523 8211; www.hostelsclub.com). Reserve well in advance.

Senior citizens Venice is a popular destination for older travellers although, due to the limited transport system you must be prepared for lots of walking. The best deals are available through tour operators who specialize in tours for senior citizens. There are reductions for entry to museums for EU citizens over 65 years of age.

Being there

TOURIST OFFICES

Head Office
Palazzina del Santi
Giardinetti Reale
San Marco
☎ 041 529 8711;
www.turismovenezia.it

Branches
International Arrivals Hall
Marco Polo airport
☎ 041 541 5887

Ferrovia Santa Lucia (train station)
☎ 041 529 8711
Piazza San Marco 71
☎ 041 529 8711
Piazzale Roma
☎ 041 529 8711
Gran Viale Santa Maria Elisabetta 6
(Lido office)
☎ 041 541 5721

MONEY
The euro (€) is the official currency of Italy. Banknotes are issued in denominations of 5, 10, 20, 50, 100, 200 and 500 euros; coins in denominations of 1, 2, 5, 10, 20 and 50 cents, and 1 and 2 euros.

TIPS/GRATUITIES

Yes ✓ No ✗		
Restaurants (if service not included)	✓	10–15%
Cafés/bars (if service not included)	✓	€1 minimum
Tour guides	✓	€1 minimum
Water-taxis	✓	10%
Chambermaids	✓	€2
Porters	✓	€1
Toilet attendants	✓	50c minimum

POSTAL SERVICES
Most post offices open Mon–Fri from 8–2. Some also open on Saturday morning. The main post office *(ufficio postale)* at Palazzo delle Poste, Salizzada del Fontego dei Tedeschi (near the Rialto Bridge) is open Mon–Sat 8–7 (www.poste.it). You can also buy stamps *(francobolli)* at tobacconists *(tabacchi)*, idenitified with a large 'T' sign.

TELEPHONES

Public telephones take coins, tokens *(gettone)* or phone cards *(schede telfoniche)* that can be bought from Telecom Italia (TI) offices (the state telephone company) or *tabacchi*, bars and newsstands. You have to break off the marked corner of the phonecard before use.

International dialling codes

From Venice to:
UK: 00 44
Germany: 00 49
Netherlands: 00 31
Spain: 00 34
USA: 00 1

Emergency telephone numbers

National Police (Polizia dello Stato): 113
City Police (Carabinieri): 112
Fire (Vigili del Fuoco): 115
Ambulance (Ambulanza): 118 or 041 523 0000

EMBASSIES AND CONSULATES

UK: ☎ 041 505 5990
USA in Milan: ☎ 02 290351
Germany: ☎ 041 523 7675

Netherlands: ☎ 041 528 3416
Spain: ☎ 041 523 3254

HEALTH ADVICE

Sun advice The sunniest (and hottest) months are June, July and August. You are advised to use a strong sunblock and avoid the midday sun.
Drugs Prescription and non-prescription drugs and medicines are available from a pharmacy *(farmacia)*, distinguished by a green cross.
Safe water Tap water is generally safe to drink unless marked *acqua non potabile*. Drink plenty of water in hot weather.

PERSONAL SAFETY

To help prevent crime:

- Do not carry more cash around with you than you need
- Beware of pickpockets in markets, tourist sights or crowded places
- The main police station, at Via San Nicoladi 22, Marghera (☎ 041 271 5772, 041 271 5586) has a special department to deal with visitors' problems

ELECTRICITY

The power supply is 220 volts, but is suitable for 240-volt appliances. Sockets accept two-round-pin Continental-style plugs. US visitors should bring a voltage transformer.

OPENING HOURS

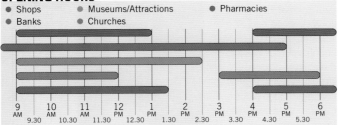

Many shops and supermarkets also open outside the times shown above, especially in summer. Most food shops close on Wednesday afternoons, while many other shops close Monday mornings (except in summer), and may close Saturday afternoon; most shops close on Sundays. Some churches are permanently closed except during services; state-run museums usually close Mondays and many stay open all day. Generally, restaurant lunch and dinner opening times are 12:30–2:30 and 7:30–10:30.

LANGUAGE

Many Venetians speak some English, but they really appreciate it when foreigners make an effort to speak Italian, however badly. It is relatively straightforward to have a go at some basics, as the words are pronounced as they are spelled. Every vowel and consonant (except 'h') is sounded and, as a general rule, the stress falls on the next-to-last syllable. Here is a basic vocabulary to help with the most essential words and expressions.

English	Italian	English	Italian
yes	*sì*	help!	*aiuto!*
no	*no*	today	*oggi*
please	*per favore*	tomorrow	*domani*
thank you	*grazie*	yesterday	*ieri*
hello	*ciao*	how much?	*quanto?*
goodbye	*arrivederci*	expensive	*caro*
goodnight	*buona notte*	open	*aperto*
sorry	*mi dispiace*	closed	*chiuso*
hotel	*albergo*	reservation	*prenotazione*
room	*camera*	rate	*tariffa*
..single/double	*..singola/doppia*	breakfast	*prima colazione*
..one/two nights	*per una/due notte/i*	toilet/bath/shower	*toilette/bagno/ doccia*
..one/two people	*..per una/due persona/e*	key	*chiave*
restaurant	*ristorante*	lunch	*pranzo/colazione*
café	*caffè*	dinner	*cena*
table	*tavolo*	starter	*il primo*
menu	*menù/carta*	main course	*il secondo*
set menu	*menù turistico*	dish of the day	*piatto del giorno*
wine list	*lista dei vini*	dessert	*dolci*
aeroplane	*aeroplano*	ferry	*traghetto*
airport	*aeroporto*	ticket	*biglietto*
train	*treno*	ticket office	*biglietteria*
bus	*autobus*	timetable	*orario*

Best places to see

1 Basilica di San Marco

www.basilicasanmarco.it

This is one of the most visited places in Europe and should not be missed – the exotic Byzantine–Venetian basilica is simply one of the world's greatest medieval buildings.

The cathedral of Venice evokes the blending of East and West that is at the heart of the Venetian character. More Eastern than European, the architecture, the decoration and the atmosphere of ancient sanctity span both the centuries and styles of Mediterranean civilization.

Originally built to house the body of St Mark, the patron saint of Venice, which had been smuggled from its tomb in Alexandria by Venetian merchants in AD828, the basilica evolved its present appearance between the 9th and 19th centuries. The basic building dates from the late 11th century, the domes from the 13th and the decoration from subsequent centuries. Much of the decoration was plundered or presented to Venice during its time of supremacy, most notably the four famous gilded horses above the main doors. Probably made in the 4th century AD, they were looted from Constantinople, when it was sacked by the Venetians during the Crusades, and stood on the outside for nearly 600 years until plundered, in turn, by the French. After the Napoleonic wars, they were restored to the basilica although, due to atmospheric pollution, the originals are now kept in a gallery inside while replicas stand in their place.

Viewing the richness of ornament outside and inside the basilica can occupy you for hours, but even the hurried visitor can admire the glowing gold of the mosaics that cover nearly half a hectare (1 acre) of the vaulting or examine them more closely from the galleries. If you don't have time to go inside, or the teeming crowds prove too much for you, spend a few minutes taking in the exterior details. The central door's Romanesque carvings dating from the 13th century are considered the exterior's greatest treasures. Superbly carved, they show the earth, the seas and animals on the underside, with the virtues and the beatiudes on the outer face and the Zodiac and labours of the month on the inner.

If you have more time to go inside make sure you see the elaborate gold Byzantine altarpiece, the Pala d'Oro. Encrusted with over 2,600 pearls, rubies, emeralds and other precious stones, it was begun in the 10th century but not completed until 1342.

The Basilica has been the cathedral of Venice only since 1807. Before that time it had been the shrine of San Marco and the chapel of the Doge, while the church of San Pietro di Castello in the far east of the city (➤ 110) had been the cathedral, an arrangement to minimize the influence of the Papacy on the affairs of Venice.

✚ 20J ✉ Piazza San Marco 1 ☎ 041 270 8311 ⚙ Oct–Apr Mon–Sat 9:45–5, Sun 2–5; Nov–Mar Mon–Sat 9:45–5, Sun 2–4 ✋ Basilica free. Museo Marciano, Treasury and Pala d'Oro inexpensive 🍴 Piazza San Marco (€€€)
🚤 Vallaresso/San Zaccaria

2 Canal Grande

This must be one of the best places in the world to take a boat trip. Take in all the city's finest palaces and scenes of Venetian life along the way.

Following the course of an original creek through the muddy islands of the lagoon, the serpentine canal sweeps in two great curves from what is now the Santa Lucia rail station to the Basin of San Marco. Its width varies from 40–70m (130–230ft), has a maximum depth of 5.5m (18ft) and is crossed by four main bridges – the Ponte della Constituzione, the Scalzi, the Rialto and the Accademia – and seven *traghetto* (ferry gondola) routes.

Travelling eastwards along the Canal, some of the principal buildings between the station and the Rialto Bridge are, on the left, the Scalzi, San Geremia and San Marcuola and Ca' Labia (Tiepolo frescoes), Ca' Vendramin-Calergi (the Municipal Casino in winter) and the Ca' d'Oro (museum and art gallery). On the right are San Simeone Piccolo and San Stae, Fondaco dei Turchi (Natural History Museum), Ca' Pesaro (Museums of Modern Art and Oriental Art) and Ca' Favretto (Hotel San Cassiano) – and then the fish, fruit and vegetable markets just before the Rialto Bridge.

Between the Rialto and the Accademia bridges are, on the left, the church of San Samuele and the Ca' Mocenigo (not to be confused with the Palazzo Mocenigo, which is open to the public) and Palazzo Grassi; on the right, Ca' Rezzonico (museum of 18th-century arts) – then, at the Accademia Bridge, the Accademia Gallery in the former church and *scuola* (school) of Santa Maria della Carità.

Between the Accademia Bridge and the Basin of San Marco are, on the left, Ca' Barbaro, Ca' Grande (Prefecture of Police), Ca' Gritti-Pisani (Gritti Palace Hotel), Ca' Tiepolo (Europa e Regina Hotel) and the buildings around Piazza San Marco.

On the right are the church of Santa Maria della Salute and the palaces of Ca' Venier dei Leoni (housing the superb collection at the Peggy Guggenheim Collection of Modern Art), Ca' Dario (its façade richly inlaid with multi-coloured marble) and, at the extreme end, the Dogana di Mare (the Customs House).

✚ 1D–18K 🚤 1, 82, 2

3 Gallerie dell'Accademia

www.gallerieaccademia.org

This is the initimate home to some of the best of Venetian art spanning the 14th to the 18th centuries, from Byzantine to baroque.

The most famous and comprehensive collection of Venetian painting is housed in this former church, monastery and *scuola* at the Dorsoduro side of the wooden Accademia Bridge (one of the four crossing points of the Canal Grande). Most paintings come from palaces and churches in the city, and although it would have been more appropriate to see them in their original settings, here they are grouped in galleries and are well lit.

Usually some galleries are closed for various reasons, but there is always enough on display to delight and even sometimes to cause visual and mental indigestion – try to avoid Sundays, which are particularly busy. Highlights include Giovanni Bellini's *Madonna Enthroned* and Carpaccio's *The Presentation of Jesus* in Room II; Giorgione's *Tempest* and Bellini's *Madonna of the Trees* in Room V; Titian's *St John the Baptist* in Room VI; three magnificent paintings by Veronese in Room XI; the Accademia's only Canaletto and six charming 18th-century *Scenes from Venetian Life* by Longhi in Room XVII; and Carpaccio's enchanting series of paintings illustrating *The Legend of St Ursula*, portraying the clothes and settings of 15th-century Venice, in Room XXI.

🕂 16K ✉ Campo della Carità, Dorsoduro 1023
☎ 041 520 0345 🕑 Mon 8:15–2, Tue–Sun
8:15–7:15 (last entrance at 6:45) Expensive; a
combined ticket for the Accademia, the Ca' d'Oro
and Museo d'Arte Orientale is a good buy
🚤 Accademia

Palazzo Ducale

www.museiciviciveneziani.it

The palace, a vast, grandiose civic building, is the cream of Italy's Gothic constructions.

Venice was governed from the Doges' Palace for a thousand years, and it still dominates the city. The pink palace, with its white colonnades that can be seen across the water from the Basin of San Marco, looks much as it did when it replaced an earlier building in the 14th century, except that its pillars seem foreshortened because the level of the surrounding path has been raised. Here the elected doge of Venice held his court and presided over a system of councils, designed to prevent any one self-interested faction from seizing power. Once, when this failed, the over-ambitious Doge Marin Falier was convicted of treason and beheaded at the top of the new marble staircase in the palace courtyard and his portrait replaced by a black cloth.

Visitors to the palace can marvel at the richly decorated council chambers on the second floor,

their walls and ceilings painted by the leading Venetian painters, including Tintoretto, whose *Paradise* is one of the largest old-master paintings in the world. It graces the wall of the Sala del Maggior Consiglio (Great Council Chamber), a vast hall designed to seat 1,700 citizens who had the right to vote in the council. Have a look at the Armoury, with some 2,000 weapons and suits of armour.

From the Palace itself, the Ponte dei Sospiri (Bridge of Sighs) crosses a canal to the prison and the notorious, waterlogged dungeons below water level known as *pozzi* (the wells). You can join guided tours through the palace and the prison and also special tours of the 'secret rooms' (in English, French and Italian). This includes the interrogation rooms and torture chamber of the State Inquisitors and the cells under the roof of the prison, from which Casanova made his dramatic escape in 1756, while serving a five-year sentence on charges involving blasphemy, magic and espionage.

The Doges' Palace is so rich in art and architectural splendours that a whole morning or afternoon could be devoted to it. When Venice is crowded, it is best to arrive early to enjoy an unhurried tour. If you visit in winter be sure to dress warmly as the Palazzo Ducale has no heating and is extremely cold.

✚ 21J ✉ Piazzetta di San Marco ☎ 041 520 9070/041 271 5911 ⏱ Apr–Oct daily 9–7; Nov–Mar 9–5 🖐 Museum Card (valid for Museo Civico Correr, Museo Archeologico Nazionale, Sala Monumentali della Biblioteca Marciana) expensive 🍴 Café (€–€€) 🛥 Vallaresso/ San Zaccaria

5 Piazza San Marco

Visitors do flock here in their thousands and it can be rather daunting, but the scale and spectacle of this piazza is breathtaking.

The Piazza San Marco is the heart of Venice. When Napoleon conquered the Venetian Republic he called it 'the most elegant drawing-room in Europe', and so it still is. At the eastern end stands the Basilica di San Marco with its Byzantine domes; to one side its campanile, the Piazzetta outside the Doges' Palace and the Basin of San Marco; to the other the Clock Tower and the Piazzetta dei Leoncini, named after the red marble lions standing there. The north side of the Piazza is bounded by the Procuratie Vecchie, the former offices of the Republic's administration, with an arcade of shops below and the Caffè Quadri, once patronized by the Austrian occupiers of Venice. On the south side is the former administration building, the Procuratie Nuove, with another arcade of shops and the Caffè Florian, the favourite of Venetian patriots during the Austrian occupation, below. At the western end of the Piazza, the church of San Geminiano was demolished on Napoleon's orders, and a new arcade with a ballroom above was built (the entrance of the Correr Museum of Venetian history is now there, ➤ 82). The two granite columns near the water's edge in the Piazzetta were set up in the

12th century; one is surmounted by a stone Lion of St Mark, the other by the figure of St Theodore, the first patron saint of the city, proudly wielding shield and spear.

✚ 20J ✉ Piazza San Marco 🍴 Florian (€–€€€) and Quadri (€–€€€) 🚤 Vallaresso/San Marco

6 San Giorgio Maggiore

A tranquil haven from the bustle of San Marco, this magnificent Palladian church has tremendous views from the campanile.

The church stands on its island across the Basin of San Marco, giving Venice one of its most celebrated views. Designed by Andrea Palladio in the 16th century, it has all the majesty that the term 'Palladian' implies, and this is particularly apparent at night when the dazzling marble façade is floodlit. Originally founded in 790, the first church was destroyed by an earthquake in 1223 and not rebuilt until Palladio began work in 1559, the 1443 monastery next door taking precedence. The result was worth waiting for – one of the finest example's of Italian neoclassical architecture, complete with four-columned portico. Don't miss the choir stalls, which have some of the finest wood carving in Venice.

The interior is vast and austere, its white stone a magnificent setting for its works of art, including paintings by Tintoretto and a bronze altarpiece, *The Globe Surmounted by God the Father*, dating from the 16th century.

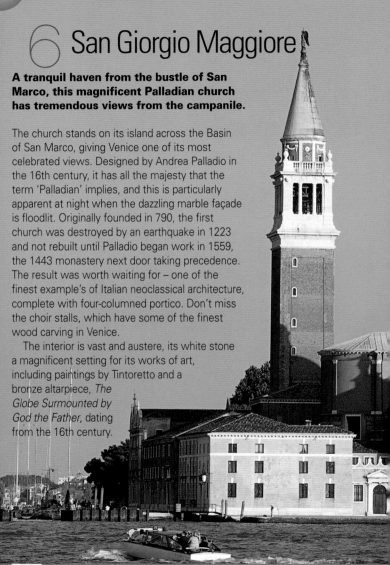

Other highlights by Tintoretto, splendidly offset by the light from the high windows, are *The Fall of Manna* and *The Last Supper* (both 1592–94), hung in the choir stalls. To the right of the choir stalls, in the Cappela dei Morti, is hung what may be Tintoretto's last work, *The Deposition* (1594).

The tall and slender campanile, ascended by an elevator, provides the best bird's-eye views of Venice. Unlike that of San Marco, it is detached from the city and can be seen as a panorama across the water.

➕ 22L ✉ Campo San Giorgio, Isola di San Giorgio Maggiore ☎ 041 522 7827 ③ May–Sep daily 9:30–12:30, 2:30–6:30; Oct–Apr 9:30–12:30, 2:30–4:30 ✋ Church free, campanile moderate 🛳 San Giorgio

7 Santi Giovanni e Paolo

Here is the resting place of more than 20 of the city's doges, buried beneath monumental tombs within a majestic Gothic church.

Called San Zanipolo by Venetians, the church stands to the north of San Marco. The largest church in Venice, it measures 101m (331ft) in length, is 38m (125ft) wide and 33m (108ft) high and was built by the Dominicans in the 14th and 15th centuries.

Despite its bulk, the red brick building is not ponderous, partly because of the cleaning of the elaborate Gothic portals at the west end and the monuments within. It is best seen on a sunny day as the interior can be dark on a dull day.

Inside, the original choir screen and stalls have not survived, leaving the nave light and airy. The church is commonly called the Pantheon of Doges, and around the walls stand magnificent monuments to doges and, among other notables, the Venetian general Marcantonio Bragadin, who was flayed alive by the Turks when they captured Cyprus in 1571. Not only does a fresco on the monument depict this, but the flayed skin, which was stolen from Constantinople, lies in a small sarcophagus. His death was avenged at the Battle of Lepanto by Doge Sebastiano Venier, whose fine bronze statue also stands in the church.

➕ 10F ✉ Campo Santi Giovanni e Paolo, Castello 6363 ☎ 041 523 5913 🕓 Daily 7:30–12:30, 3:30–7. Closed during services 🖐 Inexpensive 🍴 Rosa Salva bar for coffee nearby (€) 🚢 Fondamenta Nove/Ospedale Civile

8 Santa Maria Gloriosa dei Frari

www.basilicadeifrari.it

Another superb Gothic building and Venice's second largest church, it is filled with magnificent paintings, monuments and ornate woodwork.

This church is Venice's second largest and has some impressive statistics. Built of brick, it is huge: 98m (322ft) long, 46m (151ft) wide and 28m (92ft) high, and dates from the 14th and 15th centuries. Reached through a maze of streets, it was the Franciscans' Venetian powerbase, originally founded in 1250. The church stands on the far side of the Canal Grande and is almost as large as Santi Giovanni e Paolo but has a wholly different character. The choir screen and stalls remain in place and the nave is

shadowed and sombre, as are the vast and elaborate monuments. Memorable among these is the open-doored vast white pyramid (1827) containing the

heart of the 19th-century sculptor Antonio Canova. He designed it as a monument to the great Venetian painter Titian (*d*1576), who, in fact, is buried across the aisle under a dramatic 19th-century statue.

Two paintings are the particular glories of the Frari. One is Titian's huge *The Assumption* (1516–18), still in the position for which it was painted above the high altar. The other is *The Madonna and Child* by Bellini in the sacristy, one of the loveliest paintings in Venice.

Like Santi Giovanni e Paolo (➤ 48–49), the Frari can easily occupy an hour or so of your time, particularly those with a passion for architecture, painting and sculpture.

✚ 15G ✉ Campo dei Frari, San Polo 3072 ☎ 041 275 0462 or 041 275 0494 🕒 Mon–Sat 9–6, Sun 1–6 👜 Inexpensive 🚢 San Tomà

Santa Maria della Salute

This great baroque church stands proudly at the entrance to the Grand Canal, one of the most imposing landmarks in the city.

Like the Redentore (▶ 151), this church was built to give thanks for the ending of a plague, but in the following century. The great domed church has sometimes been seen as the hostess of the city, welcoming visitors; as the novelist Henry James wrote: 'like some great lady on the threshold of her salon…with her domes and scrolls, her scalloped buttresses and statues forming a pompous crown,

and her wide steps disposed on the ground like the train of a robe'. After dark, a walk through the alleys of Dorsoduro can suddenly end on the brilliantly floodlit steps of the Salute beneath its gleaming bulk, the water below dancing with reflected light.

The magnificent baroque interior is more restrained and somewhat austure in comparision to the exuberant exterior. You can view an early Titian, *The Descent of the Holy Spirit* (1550), third on the left. Other fine paintings can be found in the sacristy, with eight more Titians and Tintoretto's magnificent *Marriage Feast at*

Cana (1561). Look for his self-portrait – the artist is depicted as the first Apostle on the left. You have to pay an admission charge to see these paintings, but it's worth it.

Venetians still come to the church on 21 November, the feast day of the Salute, to give thanks for good health.

✚ 18K ✉ Campo della Salute, Dorsoduro, near the eastern end of the Grand Canal ☎ 041 522 5558 ⏰ Apr–Sep daily 9–12, 3–6:30; Oct–Mar 9–12, 3–5:30. Sacristy Mon–Sat 10–11:30, 3–5, Sun 3–5 ✋ Church free; sacristy inexpensive 🚤 Salute

10 Scuola Grande di San Rocco

www.scuolagrandesanrocco.it

Drawn in by the mastery of the cycle of 54 paintings by Tintoretto, you won't be disappointed by the stunning ornate interior.

This is the largest and grandest of the *scuole*, standing close to the church of the Frari. It was founded in honour of St Roch, a saint who dedicated his life to the care of the sick. It is most celebrated for its great series of powerful paintings by Tintoretto depicting Biblical scenes, a monumental achievement covering the walls and ceilings of this magnificent *scuola*. It is best to start by heading up the great staircase to the Sala dell'Albergo, off the main hall, to see the works in the order Tintoretto painted them. The room is dominated by the powerful *Crucifixion* (1565), one of the greatest paintings in the world. In the main upper hall you will find striking ceiling

paintings depicting scenes from the Old Testament. The vast scenes on the walls epict episodes from the New Testament, showing Tintoretto's departure from contemporary ideas with the use of colour, form and light.

Coming back downstairs to the Ground Floor Hall you will find the final paintings in Tintoretto's cycle, a culmination of 23 years of work. Here the artist is at his most sublime, as seen in the execution of the *Annunciation* and the *Flight into Egypt*. These reflect the artist's late style, and the use of dramatic light is revolutionary for its time. In addition to these superb paintings and the ornate interior, look for the beautiful carvings below the paintings, works by 17th-century sculptor Francesco Pianta.

🚹 15G ✉ Campo San Rocco, San Polo 3052 ☎ 041 523 4864 🕐 Apr–Oct daily 9–5:30; Nov–Mar 10–4 ✋ Moderate 🚇 San Tomà

SCVOLA GRANDE
DI SAN ROCCO
S|R

Best things to do

Good places to have lunch

Ai Corazzieri (€–€€)
Get away from the crowds at this pleasant trattoria and pizzeria with outside dining.
✉ Salizzada dei Corazzieri, Castello 3839 ☎ 041 528 9859

Al Bacco (€€)
If it's a sunny day take advantage of the pretty courtyard garden at this locals' haunt with great fish and seafood.
✉ Fondamenta Capuzine, Cannaregio 3054 ☎ 041 717 493

Al Bottegon (€)
This is one of the best places to have lunch. Snack on excellent panini, washed down by great wine and while you linger catch up on your people-watching.
✉ Fondementa Nani, Dorsoduro 992 ☎ 041 523 0034

Alla Maddelena (€€)
Lovely island setting for a tasty lunch; the perfect antidote to the busy city. Try the tasty duck.
✉ Mazzorbo 7c ☎ 041 730 151

Busa alla Torre (€€)

When you've bought the glass take a break in this Murano restaurant renowned for its fish.

✉ Campo Santo Stefano, Murano 3 ☎ 041 739 662

Il Refolo (€€)

Pleasantly situated by a quiet canal, this is a popular spot for a lunch of pizza, pasta or salad. Good house wine and scrumptious desserts.

✉ Campo San Giacomo dell'Orio, Santa Croce 1459 ☎ 041 524 0016

Locanda Cipriani (€€€)

You will need a fat wallet to eat here, but the walled garden on the island of Torcello is a gorgeous place to have lunch and the food is memorable.

✉ Piazza Santa Fosca, Torcello 29 ☎ 041 730 150

Mistrà (€–€€)

Located on the island of Giudecca in a converted warehouse, there are great views towards the lagoon, plus good fish and seafood dishes.

✉ Fondamenta San Giacomo, Giudecca ☎ 041 522 0743

Nico (€)

Must be one of the nicest places to pause and enjoy possibly the best ice cream in the city – right on the watefront. Also sells snacks.

✉ Fondamenta Zattere, Dorsoduro ☎ 041 522 5293

Vecio Fritolin (€)

You can have a snack lunch here; very much a local *bacaro* with a lovely atmosphere. Or you can go the whole hog with a full meal of flame-grilled fish.

✉ Calle della Regina, Santa Croce 2262 ☎ 041 522 2281

Stunning views

Arriving – by water taxi or *vaporetto* (➤ 27, 28) from the airport; the ideal way to get your first glimpse of Venice.

Campanile – Venice's highest building commands great views of the city and the lagoon (➤ 80–81).

Fondamente Nuove – come here to get a fine aspect of San Michele across the lagoon (➤ 165).

From a boat on the Grand Canal – surely the best way to see the beautiful *palazzi* of Venice (➤ 72–73).

Giudecca – the silhouetted buildings of the Dorsoduro look wonderful from the Campo del Redentore on the island of Giudecca (➤ 147).

Island of San Giorgio Maggiore – the best place to get a view of the city is from the campanile of the church (➤ 46–47).

Ponte dell'Accadmia – terrific views down the Grand Canal and also towards the church of Santa Maria della Salute (➤ 52–53).

Ponte di Rialto – just the place to get the a bird's-eye view of the life on the Grand Canal (➤ 132).

Dogana di Mare – at this vantage point in Dorsoduro you get a fine view across the mouth of the Grand Canal to the north and the Canale della Giudecca to the south (➤ 144).

Torcello – climb the bell tower of the cathedral of Santa Maria Assunta for lagoon views (➤ 167).

Best façades

Basilica di San Marco with its fine mosaics and rich ornamentation (➤ 36–37).

Ca' d'Oro may not be as spectacular as it once was but it still impresses (➤ 118).

Madonna dell'Orto, tucked away in Cannaregio, has a graceful red-brick and marble Gothic façade (➤ 120).

Palazzo Ducale is an amazing pink palace with white colonnades presiding regally over Piazza San Marco (➤ 42–43).

San Giorgio Maggiore, one of Palladio's greatest churches, cannot fail to dazzle with its stunning marble exterior (➤ 46–47).

Prettiest squares

Campo San Giacomo dell'Orio (➤ 133).

Campo San Polo (➤ 130).

Campo Santa Margherita (➤ 143).

Campo Santa Maria Formosa (➤ 102).

Campo Santo Stefano (➤ 81).

Best churches

Madonna dell'Orto
This church has a lovely, peaceful setting and paintings by Tintoretto, who is also buried here (➤ 120).

San Giacomo dell'Orio
Most Venetian churches are old, but none look or feel quite as venerable as sleepy San Giacomo (➤ 133).

San Giovanni in Bragora
The composer Vivaldi was baptized in this tiny church, which contains a magnificent high altarpiece and other fine paintings (➤ 108–109).

Santi Giovanni e Paolo
This is the burial place of many eminent Venetians, including several doges, and contains numerous magnificent tombs (➤ 48–49).

Santa Maria Gloriosa dei Frari
Venice's second largest church, filled with masterpieces by Titian, Giovanni Bellini and others (➤ 50–51).

Santa Maria dei Miracoli
The most beautiful exterior of any Venetian church, thanks to its lovely marble façades (➤ 123).

Santa Maria della Salute
The great domes of the Salute are one of Venice's most recognizable landmarks (➤ 52–53).

San Sebastiano
The parish church of the painter Veronese, who provided many of its ceiling paintings and other sumptuous decoration (➤ 152–153).

Santo Stefano
A glorious wooden ceiling is the highlight of the airy Santo Stefano
(► 89).

San Zaccaria
A wonderful façade, a lovely Bellini altarpiece and secret little crypt
distinguish this fascinating church (► 110–111).

Speciality shops and markets

MASKS AND ACCESSORIES

Balocoloc

Silvana Martin is a wonderfully original milliner, who produces all the hats sold in this tiny shop. You'll find brimmed hats, pull-ons and berets in a myriad of colours; designs change each season.

✉ Calle Lunga, Santa Croce 2134 ☎ 041 524 0551 🚤 San Silvestro

Mondo Novo

This little gem is one of the most famous mask shops in the city. It combines the traditional with the modern and the workmanship is highly skilled, producing a beautiful end product.

✉ Ria Terrà Canal, Dorsoduro 3063 ☎ 041 528 7344 🚤 Ca' Rezzonico

Tragicomica

Here you can gain an insight into the origins of the Carnevale; all the 18th-century characters are represented through fantastic craftsmanship.

✉ Calle dei Nomboli, San Polo 2800 ☎ 041 721 102 🚤 San Tomà

PAPER AND STATIONERY

Ebrû

A particularly elegant stock of hand-printed paper and silk is offered by Alberto Valese-Ebrû, who was at the forefront of the revival in Venetian marbled paper in the 1970s. Gorgeous gifts – notebooks, frames, boxes and paper in beautiful hues.

✉ Campiello Santo Stefano, San Marco 3471 ☎ 041 523 8830
🚤 Accademia

Legatoria Piazzesi

This is one of the last workshops in the city to use the traditional wood-block method of printing to hand print beautiful marbled paper, books and stationery. It's expensive but it is stunning and you can always buy a single sheet to take home as a souvenir.

✉ Campiello Feltrina, San Marco 2511 ☎ 041 522 1202 🚤 Giglio

GLASS BEADS

Perle e Dintorni

Superb selection of beads that can be made into necklaces, earrings and bracelets on the spot. Also sell ready-to-wear pieces.

✉ Calle della Mandola, San Marco 3740 ☎ 041 520 5068 🚤 Sant'Angelo

MARKETS

Pescheria

Not for the weak-stomached but an experience nevertheless. This fish market, by the Grand Canal, is worth a look for its squid, crabs and strange-looking fish. The stallhaolders will gut, slice and prepare your purchases for you.

✉ Fondamenta dell'Olio, San Polo 🕐 Tue–Sat 8–1 🚤 Rialto

Rialto

A 1,000-year-old trading station and although most produce is shipped from the mainland, it's good stuff.

✉ Ruga dei Orefici, San Polo 🕐 Mon–Sat 8–1 🚤 Rialto

Best paintings and picture cycles

Gentile Bellini and others
The Miracles of the True Cross (1494–1510): various leading artists contributed to this wonderful narrative fresco cycle in the Gallerie dell'Accademia.

Giandomenico Tiepolo
Highlight's of Tiepolo's frescoes displayed at the Ca'Rezzonico (➤ 142) are the *Punchinello* (Mr Punch) series and the modern *Mondo Novo*, painted for his own home between 1759 and 1797.

Giorgione
The Tempest (*c*1500): a star turn in the Gallerie dell'Accademia
(➤ 40–41) and one of the city's most mysterious paintings.

Giovanni Bellini
*Madonna and Child between Saints Nicholas, Peter, Mark and
Benedict* (1488): a side chapel in the church of Santa Maria
Gloriosa dei Frari (➤ 50–51) contains the most beautiful of Bellini's
several Venetian altarpieces.

Jacopo Robusti Tintoretto
Crucifixion (1565): the highlight of more than 50 paintings by
Tintoretto in the Scuola Grande di San Rocco (➤ 54–55).

Paradiso (1588–92): at 140sq m (1,500sq ft), this masterpiece in
the Palazzo Ducale (➤ 42–43) is the world's single largest oil
painting.

Tiziano Vecello (Titian)
Assumption (1516–18): the majestic high altarpiece of Santa Maria
Gloriosa dei Frari (➤ 50–51).

Madonna di Ca' Pesaro (1526): charming portraits and
compositional daring fill the second of Titian's masterpieces in
the Frari church (➤ 50–51).

Vittore Carpaccio
Scenes from the Life of St Ursula (1500): quirky and lovely
incidental details fill Carpaccio's fresco cycle in the Gallerie
dell'Accademia (➤ 40–41).

Scenes from the Life of St George, St Tryphon and St Jerome
(1508): another ravishing fresco cycle from Carpaccio, this time
hidden away in the Scuola di San Giorgio degli Schiavoni (➤ 112).

Places to take the children

Boat trips
There's plenty to see on a *vaparotto* ride along the Grand Canal or out to one of the islands. Arriving by boat from the airport is an exciting experience (➤ 27).

Glass-blowing
Watching the glassblowers at work, even at one of the demonstration furnaces in the city, is enthralling and children need no persuading to start collecting little – and inexpensive – glass animals (➤ Murano, 162–163).

Gondolas
It does cost a lot, but it's by the boat, not by the person, so a family of up to five can be accommodated (➤ 27).

Islands
Take a trip to Murano (➤ 162–163) to see the glassblowing, Burano (➤ 160–161) for the pretty houses or Torcello (➤ 167) for a peaceful walk. Don't forget the smaller islands either; try Sant'Erasmo, where you can walk, cycle, take a picnic or head for the little beach.

Lido
The Lido offers a chance to swim or play on the beach. You can rent bicycles or pedaloes (small pedal-operated boats) from outlets on the front. Look for the public beaches; many are owned by hotels and are private (➤ 162).

Museums
For would-be historians try the following: the Museo Storico Navale (➤ 104), with its beautifully constructed model ships and the displays of the glories of Venice's maritime past; the Palazzo Ducale (➤ 42–43), where you'll need to be brave to venture into the palace's dungeons with the spine-tingling torture chambers.

Puntolaguna

Plenty of interactives in this multimedia centre devoted to ecology and the state of the lagoon. Workshops for children (➤ 84).

Swimming

The Piscina Comunale Sant' Alvise (Calle del Capitello, Cannaregio 3163 ☎ 041 713 567) offers swimming sessions and lessons as well as a mini-pool for little kids. You have to wear a swimming cap in the water and flip flops from the changing rooms to the water.

Towers

Get a bird's-eye view of Venice from the top of the Campanile in Piazza San Marco (➤ 80–81) or the church on the island of San Giorgio Maggiore (➤ 46–47).

Watching the pigeons

Love them or hate them, you can't avoid them in Piazza San Marco (➤ 44–45). It's best not to feed them as they can be a nuisance. Just have a look.

a boat trip along the Canal Grande

Venice's main thoroughfare is the Grand Canal, thronged with gondolas, waterbuses and motor launches and lined with aristocratic *palazzi*.

Leaving from San Marco Vallareso, the boat passes Harry's Bar on the right (➤ 94) and then the 17th-century customs house (➤ 144) on the left. You will see the baroque church of Santa Maria della Salute also to the left (➤ 52–53), followed by the marble façade of the Palazzo Dario built in 1487. Next on the left is the oddly squat building, the Palazzo Venier dei Leoni, which is now home to the Collezione Peggy Guggenheim (➤ 144). Shortly before the Accademia footbridge, constructed in 1932, is the Palazzo Barbaro. Beyond the bridge, on the left, is the Gallerie dell'Accademia (➤ 40–41).

After the Accademia bridge are two *palazzi* on the left, Palazzo Querini, former home to the British Consulate, and Palazzo Loredan dell'Ambasciatore with its fine Gothic façade. Just beyond the next waterbus stop, on the left, is Robert Browning's former home, Ca' Rezzonico (➤ 142), now a museum of 18th-century Venice. Look to either side for more striking *palazzi*, including the massive Palazzo Giustinian on the left, where Wagner composed the second act of *Tristan and Isolde* in 1858. Crowds get off at the next stop, San Tomà, giving you the chance to look across to see Palazzo Mocenigo (➤ 131), where Byron lived with his unruly mistress, Margherita Cogni and a menagerie of pets including a monkey, a fox and a wolf. The next bridge, the famous Rialto (➤ 132), is lined with shops. Round the corner is the Pescheria on the left and the striking Ca' d'Oro (➤ 118) on the right.

Farther on, all on the left, are baroque Ca' Pesaro (➤ 130), the baroque church of San Stae (➤ 135) and the magnificent Renaissance Palazzo Vendramin Calergi, where Wagner died in 1883. The boat stops at San Marcuola, and you can see the church with its unfinished brick façade. Across the water are the 17th-century Fondaco dei Turchi (Turkish) warehouses. The final bridge is Ponte dei Scalzi.

Distance Nearly 4km (2.5 miles)

Time About 40 mins by *vaporetto* – No 1 stops at every stop, No 82 stops at six. You can rent a quicker water taxi or a gondola (which will be much slower and very expensive), or take one of the organized tours from the Riva degli Schiavoni near Piazza San Marco.

Start point Vallareso (San Marco) *vaporetto* stop 🚩 19K

End point Ferrovia *vaporetto* stop 🚩 3D

Lunch After your trip wander over the Ponte degli Scalzi into the Santa Croce district, an area where you will find better value for your money than on the main tourist track

Best places to stay

Calcina (€€)

John Ruskin stayed here while writing *The Stones of Venice*. The 29 rooms are attractively furnished with period touches. It offers good value and one of the best settings for the price.

✉ Fondamenta Zattere ai Gesuati, Dorsoduro 780 ☎ 041 520 6466; www.lacalcina.com 🚢 Zattere

Casa Verardo (€€)

This 16th-century *palazzo* has a Residenza d'Epoca rating, only applied to hotels located in historically important buildings; this says it all. Bedrooms are big, with hand-painted furniture, rich textiles and wonderfully squishy sofas. Outside, the courtyard is a lovely place to put your feet up and is just a five-minute walk from Piazza San Marco.

✉ Campo Santi Filippo e Giacomo, Castello 4756 ☎ 041 528 6138; www.casaverardo.it 🚢 San Zaccaria

Cipriani (€€€€)

This ranks as one of the world's greatest hotels, with a price to match. If it's luxury, privacy and impeccable service you want, you will get it here on the island of Giudecca. It has a magnificent open-air swimming pool and the famous Locanda Cipriani restaurant (► 59). Shuttle boat service to San Marco.

✉ Giudecca 10 ☎ 041 520 7744; www.cipriani.it 🚢 Zitelle

Danieli (€€€€)

Guests here have included Dickens, Wagner and Proust. The original building has atmosphere and sumptuous style in its public rooms. You should reserve a room in the old building rather than the newer annexe. There are 230 rooms and 11 suites to choose from. The food is good and service is great.

✉ Riva degli Schiavoni 4196 ☎ 041 522 6480; www.luxury collection.com 🚢 San Zaccaria

Gritti Palace (€€€€)

The Gritti was built as a *palazzo* in the 15th century and sumptuously converted while retaining its original style. In summer, its main delight is the open-air Terrazza del Doge, where meals are served beside the Grand Canal. A courtesy launch takes you to the hotel group's facilities on the Lido.

✉ Campo Santa Maria del Giglio, San Marco 2467 ☎ 041 794 611; www.starwoodhotels.com 🚤 Giglio

La Galleria (€€)

A simple, old-fashioned style of hotel that's welcoming and comfortable and good value considering its location. Twelve rooms in all but reserve well in advance to get one of the larger ones overlooking the canal.

✉ Campo della Carità, Dorsoduro 878/A ☎ 041 523 2489; www.hotelgalleria.it 🚤 Accademia

Locanda Armizo (€–€€)

Excellent value, just a stone's throw from the Rialto, Locanda Armizo is tucked away beneath a *sottoportego* (passage under a building) in the corner of Campo San Silvestro. Prices are per room, not per person – some sleep up to five – making this a great choice for families.

✉ Campo San Silvestro, San Polo 1104 ☎ 041 520 6473; www.armizo.com 🚤 San Silvestro

Exploring

Venice is divided into six *sestieri* (districts): to the north of the Grand Canal, San Marco is in the centre with Castello to the east and Cannaregio to the west. South of the Canal, running from east to west, lie Dorsoduro, San Polo and Santa Croce.

Each area has its own points of interest and individual character. The most expensive area to stay and eat out in is around San Marco. This district and the streets leading to the Rialto Bridge and along the waterfront can get very busy at times.

Without a good map it is easy to get disorientated, although it adds to the fun, giving you a chance to see less well-known parts of the city. For a more relaxed and cheaper option Dorsoduro, with its fine churches and picturesque squares, is a good bet. Many people choose to stay towards Castello, which offers some inexpensive small hotels and restaurants.

San Marco and San Giorgio Maggiore

The *sestiere*, or district, of San Marco is the historic heart of Venice, home to Piazza San Marco (St Mark's Square),

SAN MARCO

SAN GIORGIO MAGGIORE

which in turn is home to the Basilica di San Marco (St Mark's), the city's ancient religious centre, and to the Palazzo Ducale (Doges' Palace), Venice's political focus for over 700 years.

On its northern edge, San Marco also contains the Rialto, the germ of the orginal city, on whose prominent sandbar the first real settlers created homes, probably in the fifth century. It also contains many of the city's designer stores, as well as the Fenice opera house and many of its leading hotels and restaurants. Its western limits, especially around Campo Santo Stefano, Campo Manin and Campo Sant'Angelo, are much quieter, while across the water the Isola di San Giorgio Maggiore is a tiny world unto itself, with some lovely views.

BASILICA DI SAN MARCO
Best places to see, pages 36–37.

CAFFÈ FLORIAN
This charming, frescoed café has been in business since 1720 and serves some of the most expensive coffee and hot chocolate in the city. But how could you resist sitting at an outside table in the very heart and soul of the city, the Piazza di San Marco? When established by Floriano Francesoni it was known as Venezia Trionfante and by the early 1800s was a Venetian favourite, favoured by Lord Byron and German poet Goethe.
www.caffeflorian.com

✚ 20J ✉ Piazza San Marco 56

☎ 041 520 5641 🕘 May–Oct daily 9:30am–midnight; Nov–Apr Thu–Tue 10am–10:30pm 🚤 Vallaresso (San Marco)

CAMPANILE DI SAN MARCO
The bell tower rises 99m (325ft) above the piazza, the tallest building in Venice. The original collapsed in 1902 in a heap of rubble but was rebuilt over the next 10 years. It is entered through the beautiful little loggetta, built in the 16th century by Jacopo Sansovino and restored after it was destroyed in 1902. An internal elevator takes visitors to the gallery surrounding the belfry, which has panoramic views of the city, the lagoon and, on clear days, the Veneto and the Alps.

✚ 20J ✉ Piazza San Marco
☎ 041 522 4064 🕐 Jul–Aug
daily 9–9; Apr–Jun, Sep, Oct
9–7; Nov–Mar 9:30–3:45
🎫 Expensive 🚤 San
Zaccaria/Vallaresso (San Marco)

CAMPO SANTO STEFANO

This is one of Venice's finest
squares, busy and popular
but big enough to absorb
the crowds, the local
children, the students and
backpackers who meet up
here. At its north end is the
church of Santo Stefano
(➤ 89), one of the city's
loveliest. There are some
good cafés, with the best
known, Paolin (➤ 95), said
to serve the best ice cream
in Venice. When you relax
here it can be difficult to
visualize it as a former
bullfighting arena, where
oxen were tied to stakes
and baited by dogs, a
practice abandoned in 1802.
✚ 17J 🚤 Accademia

CANAL GRANDE

Best places to see,
pages 38–39.

MUSEO CIVICO CORRER

The principal historical museum of the city runs above the Procuratie Nuove arcade on the west and south sides of the Piazza and is entered by a wide marble staircase at the western end. The museum is based on the 18th-century collection of Teodoro Correr, a Venetian worthy, and includes superb paintings – with some exceptional works by the Bellini family – models, costumes, footwear, books, weapons and armour, much of it captured from the Turks. Particularly sinister is the lion's mask *bocca di leone* (letter/mailbox) for written denunciations of enemies of the state. There are also relics of the *Bucintoro*, the huge, elaborate ceremonial galley used by the doges. On the first floor are the striking statues by Antonio Canova (1757–1822). The focal point is the poignant study of Daedalus and Icarus, showing the father fixing wings onto his son's arms.

The Correr is part of an ensemble of linked buildings at the western end of San Marco, which also house the city's archaelogical collections and the Biblioteca Marciana, creating one of Venice's biggest and finest museum complexes. The wonderfully stunning state rooms of the library display manuscripts and early books beneath the ceiling of allegorical Mannerist paintings.
www.museiciviciveneziani.it

✚ 19J ✉ Ala Napoleonica, Piazza San Marco 32 ☎ 041 240 5211 or call centre 041 520 9070 🕐 Apr–Oct daily 9–7; Nov–Mar 9–5 💰 Expensive but valid for Museo Archeologico Nazionale, Sala Monumnteali della Biblioteca Marciana and Palazzo Ducale 🚤 Vallaresso (San Marco)

PALAZZO CONTARINI DEL BOVOLO

This *palazzo* can unfortunately only be seen from the outside. It does, however, have a remarkable spiral staircase in its open courtyard on the Calle della Vida, close to the Campo Manin. The Bovolo Staircase (appropriately, *bovolo* means snail shell in Venetian dialect) is a remarkably delicate feat of architecture and is

best seen by moonlight.
🚹 18H 📧 Calle dei Risi,
San Marco ☎ 041 270 2464
🕐 Apr–Oct daily 10–6;
Nov–Mar Sat–Sun 10–4
✋ Moderate 🚤 Rialto

PALAZZO DUCALE
Best places to see,
pages 42–43.

PALAZZO GRASSI
This vast classic 18th-
century palace has notable
frescoes but was much
modernized in the 1980s
when it was acquired by
the Fiat car company and
used as an exhibition
space. It was bought by
the Venice authorities in
2004 and subsequently
sold to French billionaire
François Pinault, collector
and businessman. It now
presents major temporary
exhibitions, some of which
are based on the François
Pinault Collection.
www.palazzograssi.it
🚹 16J 📧 Campo San
Samuele, San Marco ☎ 041
528 7706 🕐 Wed–Mon 10–7
✋ Expensive 🚤 San Samuele

PIAZZA SAN MARCO
Best places to see, pages 44–45.

PUNTOLAGUNA
This state-of-the-art, multimedia information centre run by Venice's water authority gives information about the canal system and the lagoon, and the work going on to safeguard the future of the city and its buildings.
www.salve.it
🔲 17J ✉ Campo Santo Stefano, San Marco 2949
☎ 041 529 3582 🕐 Mon–Fri 2:30–5:30 ✋ Free
🚢 Accademia

SAN GIORGIO MAGGIORE
Best places to see, pages 46–47.

SANTA MARIA DELLA FAVA
On a back route from San Marco to the Rialto, the church of Santa Maria della Fava translates as 'St Mary of the Bean' after a popular cake called *fave dolce* (sweet beans) once produced by a nearby bakery and traditionally eaten on All Souls' Day (1 November). The church is also known as Santa Maria della Consolazione. It is a high-ceilinged 18th-century church decorated in grey statuary by Bernardi, the teacher of Canova, and has a lovely early painting by Tiepolo, *The Education of the Virgin*. A sombre contrast is the *Madonna and Child* with *St Philip Neri* by Giambattista Piazzetta.
🔲 20G ✉ Campo Rubbi, San Marco ☎ 041 522 4601
🕐 Mon–Sat 8:30–12, 4:30–6:30, Sun 8:30–12
✋ Free 🚢 Rialto

SANTA MARIA DEL GIGLIO

The carvings on the façade depict fortified cities and warships, commemorating the naval and diplomatic career of Antonio Barbaro, whose family paid for the building of the façade as his monument. The interior contains paintings by Tintoretto.

➕ 18J ✉ Campo Santa Maria del Giglio, San Marco 2452 ☎ 041 275 0462 🕐 Mon–Sat 10–5, Sun 1–5 ✋ Inexpensive ⛴ Giglio

SAN MAURIZIO

This faces the square on the well-trodden route between San Marco and the Accademia Bridge, where antiques markets are occasionally held. Rebuilt in 1806, it is a handsome, plain church in neoclassical style. In 2004, it opened as a Vivaldi exhibition centre. The cool and elegant interior now displays a series of exhibits of the life and times of the Venetian composer. You can buy all manner of CDs, tapes and DVDs relating to the composer and you can reserve concert tickets for events at Pietà (➤ 109).

➕ 17J ✉ Campo San Maurizio, San Marco ☎ 041 241 1840 🕐 Daily 9:30–8:30 ✋ Free ⛴ Giglio

SAN MOISÈ

The over-elaborate baroque façade of San Moisè commands the attention of those walking towards San Marco from the Accademia Bridge. Its interior is just as odd: the high altar appears at first sight to be a bizarre rock garden but actually turns out to be a tableau of *Moses on Mount Sinai Receiving the Tablets*. The building is a startling contrast to the smooth Bauer hotel (➤ 91) next door.

➕ 19J ✉ Campo San Moisè, San Marco 1456 ☎ 041 528 5840 🕐 Mon–Sat 10–12 ✋ Free ⛴ Vallaresso (San Marco)

a walk from San Marco

Begin in Piazza San Marco (▶ 44–45), taking in all the surrounding sights.

Facing the Basilica take the right-hand corner past the Campanile and the Palazzo Ducale to the waterfront and turn right. Continue along the waterside and turn right up Calle Vallaresso. Continue to the intersection and turn left and into Campo San Moisè with the elaborate church of San Moisè (▶ 85). Cross the bridge into Calle Larga XXII Marzo, then bear left at the end and on into Campo Santa Maria del Giglio (▶ 85). Leave the church on your right and bearing right, cross the two bridges into Campo San Maurizio, passing the church of the same name (▶ 85). Continue over the next bridge to Campo Santo Stefano (▶ 81).

This square is one of the loveliest in Venice and a great place for people-watching or lunch.

Pass the church of Santo Stefano (▶ 89) on your right and go over the bridge into Campo Sant'Angelo. Follow the canal immediately right to Calle Caotorta, cross the bridge, turn left and follow along the side of the restored Teatro la Fenice (▶ 89) out into Campo San Fantin.

Campo San Fantin is a meeting place for theatregoers, and the stunning Fenice hosts superb concerts and operas.

In the left-hand corner of the square take Calle della Verona and continue along, turning right into Calle della Mandola at the end. Proceed over the canal into Campo Manin. Cross the square, taking the left-hand corner into Salizzada San Luca and into the next square, keeping left into Calle San Luca, which takes you into Calle Fabbri, one of the city's major shopping streets. Turn left and then first right. Keep straight on past the church of San Salvador (▶ 88) into Via Due Aprile. Continue on to San Bartolomeo and turn left to the Ponte di Rialto (Rialto Bridge; ▶ 132).

Distance 2km (1.25 miles)
Time 1 hour plus stops
Start point Piazza San Marco ✚ 20J
End point Ponte di Rialto ✚ 8F
Lunch Campo Santo Stefano (▶ 81) is a charming, quiet and unspoiled square with several restaurants and cafés, including Paolin (▶ 95), one of the best places for ice cream in the city

SAN SALVADOR

This is regarded as one of the finest and most beautiful
Renaissance churches in Italy and a change from so many
Byzantine and Gothic buildings seen in Venice. It is principally
admired for its internal architecture, and its works of art feature
two paintings by Titian. *The Annunciation* is found at the end of the
right-hand aisle and if you are in any doubt as to the artist, look for
the autograph 'Tizianus, fecit, fecit'. The other, *The Transfiguration*,
hangs over the high altar.

✠ 19H ✉ Campo San Salvador, San Marco 4826 ☎ 041 523 6717, 041 296
0630 🕐 Mon–Fri 3–7 ✋ Free 🚤 Rialto

SANTO STEFANO

This large, handsome church has one of only two 'ship's keel' roofs – like a huge, inverted wooden hull – in the city (the other is in San Giacomo dell'Orio). Richly painted and decorated with inlaid, multi-coloured marble, the high Gothic interior is one of the city's loveliest. It is the only church in Venice to be built directly over a canal. The church sacristy contains paintings by Tintoretto, including the highly theatrical *Agony in the Garden* and *Last Supper*. Outside are cloisters and a leaning 16th-century campanile.

🚩 17J ✉ Campo Santo Stefano, San Marco 2774 ☎ 041 522 5061
🕐 Mon–Sat 10–5 ✋ Inexpensive ⛴ Accademia/San Samuele

TEATRO LA FENICE

The theatre was utterly destroyed by fire on 29 January 1996. More than a year later two electricians were sentenced for arson, the fire shrouded in mystery. It was not the first time the theatre had been wrecked by fire. Built by Giannantonio Silva in 1792, it had to be rebuilt after a fire in 1836. The prolonged restoration was well worth waiting for. The theatre is now a wonderful opulent reconstruction in gilt, stucco and marble and surpasses the old. In addition the equipment and sound systems are second to none. You will need to reserve well in advance for performances but you can join a tour to see all its glory.

www.teatrolafenice.it

🚩 18J ✉ Campo San Fantin, San Marco 1965
☎ 041 786 611. Call centre 041 2424 🕐 Tours only; reserve in advance by person or telephone, fax or internet. Tours last 45 mins ✋ Tours moderate
⛴ Giglio

TORRE DELL'OROLOGIO

The tower stands above the arch leading to the Mercerie shopping street close to the Basilica di San Marco. Designed by Mauro Codussi and built at the end of the 15th century, its remarkable, brightly enamelled clock face and its digital clock are linked with automata, which attract crowds in the Piazza. The exterior stone dial shows the 24 hours in Roman numerals; the interior face shows signs of the zodiac and phases of the moon. On the summit of the tower two large bronze figures known as the Mori (Moors) strike the hour. During Ascension Week and at Epiphany, figures of the Magi emerge to either side of the clock face and bow to the statue of the Madonna above it. The tower has undergone lengthly restoration work.

✚ 20H ✉ Piazza San Marco ⊛ Guided visits in English Mon–Wed at 9, 10, 11, and Thu–Sun at 1, 2, 3 (reservations compulsory – call 041 520 9070 ⛴ Vallaresso (San Marco)/San Zaccaria

HOTELS

Al Piave (€€)

Rooms are bright and colourful and a fair size for Venice in this comfortable hotel near Campo Santa Maria Formosa. The public areas are more spacious than in many Venetian hotels and include a functional space where the buffet breakfast is served.

✉ Ruga Giuffa, San Marco 4838–50 ☎ 041 528 5174; www.hotelalpiave.com 🚤 Vallaresso (San Marco)/Rialto

Bauer (€€€€)

For truly stupendous rooftop and balcony views you can't beat this luxury hotel. It's in two halves, a modern hotel with most of the rooms and the sumptuous 18th-century *palazzo* with wonderful antiques, Murano chandeliers and glorious fabrics. With 196 rooms and 60 suites this is the ultimate – saunas, Jacuzzis, health club and superb dining.

✉ Campo San Moisè, San Marco 1459 ☎ 041 520 7022; www.bauervenezia.it 🚤 Vallaresso (San Marco)

Bel Sito e Berlino (€€)

Those who wish to be in the social mainstream but cannot afford the Gritti Palace (► 74) would do well to choose the Bel Sito, just a short step away and opposite a peculiar Venetian church with a façade carved with battle rather than biblical scenes. Rooms have modern facilities, while retaining an elegant 18th and 19th century style of furnishing.

✉ Santa Maria del Giglio, San Marco 2517 ☎ 041 522 3365; www.hotelbelsito.info 🚤 Giglio

Do Pozzi (€€)

This friendly little hotel is tucked away in an alley in the heart of San Marco. Tables spill outside onto a terrace from the small reception areas and bedrooms vary in size; all are traditionally furnished. The owners are helpful and there's great attention to detail in the service provided.

✉ Via XXII Marzo, San Marco 2373 ☎ 041 520 7855; www.hotelpozzi.it 🚤 Giglio

Fiorita (€)

Among the most simple *pensioni*, the pretty Fiorita is well situated just north of Santo Stefano. It is welcoming, clean and uncomplicated; the 10 comfortable rooms (8 with private bath) have beamed ceilings.

✉ Campiello Nuovo, San Marco 3457/A ☎ 041 523 4754; www.locandafiorita.com 🚤 Accademia/Sant'Angelo

Flora (€€)

Some visitors choose the 43-roomed Flora, largely because of its lush, secluded garden and because it is conveniently close to fashionable shops. Some rooms are rather cramped, varying in size considerably – ask to see the room first. An added bonus is the friendly and helpful staff.

✉ Calle Bergamaschi, San Marco 2283/A ☎ 041 520 5844; www.hotelflora.com 🚤 Giglio

Gritti Palace (€€€€)

See page 74.

La Fenice e Des Artistes (€€)

This hotel is quite charmingly furnished and close to the Teatro La Fenice. Some of the 67 rooms have balconies. The La Taverna restaurant serves classic Venetian dishes and there is a nice courtyard area for breakfast.

✉ Campiello Fenice, San Marco 1936 ☎ 041 523 2333; www.mediumhoteles.com 🚤 Giglio

Luna Baglioni (€€€)

Venice's oldest hotel, founded in the late 15th century, has had an overhaul. Its position near the Piazza San Marco is convenient for exploring the city. The views from some of the 100 rooms are excellent. All rooms are well equipped and stylishly furnished. The public areas are sumptuous and the restaurant offers Venetian specialities.

✉ Calle dell'Ascensione, San Marco 1243 ☎ 041 528 9840; www.baglionihotels.com 🚤 Vallaresso (San Marco)

Noemi (€€)

Not far from San Marco, this traditionally styled hotel is great value for money in this expensive part of town. Not all rooms have bathrooms; check when you book; on-line booking has good offers.

✉ Calle dei Fabbri, San Marco 909 ☎ 041 523 8144; www.hotelnoemi.com ⛴ Vallaresso (San Marco)

Novecento (€€–€€€)

A nine-room boutique hotel of a type now becoming increasingly popular in Venice, the Novecento is a fusion of traditional and Middle Eastern design reflected in the furnishings. The rooms have every comfort and stylish Phillipe Starck bathrooms. Tiny courtyard and garden where breakfast is served in good weather.

✉ Calle delle Dose, Campo San Maurizio, San Marco 2683 ☎ 041 241 3765; www.locandanovecento.it ⛴ Giglio

San Samuele (€)

A budget hotel with a good location near the San Samuele *vaparetto* stop. Friendly, basic but clean and well run. Most of the 10 rooms have shared bath.

✉ Salizzada San Samuele, San Marco 3358 ☎ 041 520 5165; www.hotelsansamuele.com ⛴ San Samuele

Torino (€–€€)

Excellent value for money, this hotel is housed in a 16th-century *palazzo*. Expect solid comfort, luxurious fabrics and Venetian style; breakfast is served in a pretty dining room and there's a courtyard.

✉ Calle delle Ostreghe, San Marco 2356 ☎ 041 520 5222; www.hoteltorino.com ⛴ Giglio

RESTAURANTS

Antico Martini (€€€)

One of the city's most sophisiticated restaurants, beloved by celebs. Classic dishes such as *fegato all Veneziana con polenta* (liver with onions and polenta). Sumptuous desserts and fine wines.

✉ Campo San Fantin, San Marco 1983 ☎ 041 522 4121 🕐 Lunch, dinner. Closed Tue, dinner only Nov, Dec ⛴ Giglio

Bistrot de Venise (€€–€€€)

An atmospheric setting in a 16th-century *palazzo* and the dishes match the period. Popular with poets and the artistic crowd and there are occasional readings and exhibitions. Good wine list.

✉ Calle de Fabbri, San Marco 4685 ☎ 041 523 6651 🕐 Lunch, dinner 🚤 Rialto

Do Forni (€€€)

There are two dining rooms here. One is rustic, the other has Murano glass chandliers and opulence. Huge menu ranging from classic Italian to international dishes.

✉ Calle dei Specchieri, San Marco 468 ☎ 041 523 0663 🕐 Lunch, dinner 🚤 Vallaresso (San Marco)

Florian (€€€)

Florian, opened in 1720, is expensive but a great place for people watching. In cold weather, the interior of Florian – all faded plush and 19th-century murals – is magnificent.

✉ Piazza San Marco, San Marco 56–59 ☎ 041 520 5641 🕐 Coffee, teas snacks until midnight. Closed Wed in Dec–Feb 🚤 Vallaresso (San Marco)

Harry's Bar (€€€)

This was the original Cipriani establishment, a popular haunt of Ernest Hemingway. The food is delicious, if expensive. Try the *tagliolini verdi gratinati* (green pasta with chopped ham in a cheese sauce) with a jug of chilled Soave white wine. The bar's speciality is the Bellini – peach juice and champagne.

✉ Calle Vallaresso, San Marco 1323 ☎ 041 528 5777 🕐 Lunch, dinner 🚤 Vallaresso (San Marco)

Osteria ai Rusteghi (€)

Venice is famous for its *pannini* and *tramezzini* (filled rolls and sandwiches) and this tiny place offers well over 30 varieties, which you can enjoy with a glass or bottle of wine from the extensive list. Pleasant outdoor seting; no credit cards.

✉ Campiello del Tintor, San Marco 5513 ☎ 041 523 2205 🕐 May–Sep Mon–Fri lunch, dinner; Oct–Apr Mon–Sat lunch, dinner 🚤 Rialto

Osteria Al Bacareto (€€)

As an alternative to looking at water or boats, the passing throng is also a Venetian pleasure and some restaurants have tables out in a *campo*. A typical Venetian *trattorie*, perfect for a full meal or snack.

✉ Calle Crosera, San Marco 3447 ☎ 041 528 9336 🕐 Lunch, dinner. Closed Sat dinner and Sun 🚤 Sant'Angelo/San Samuele

Paolin (€)

This is one of the city's best cafés and ice-cream shops and one of the oldest. Nice in summer to sit at one of the outside tables and try some of the great summer fruit ice creams.

✉ Campo Santo Stefano, San Marco 296/A ☎ 041 522 5576 🕐 Lunch, dinner. Closed Mon in winter 🚤 Accademia, San Samuele

Quadri (€–€€€)

It may not be as famous as Florian (➤ opposite) but it is equally theatrical and has umpteen chandeliers and mirrors, creating a stunning effect. You can have a pricey coffee or a full meal (some good vegetarian options) overlooking the piazza.

✉ Piazza San Marco, San Marco 120/124 ☎ 041 522 2105 🕐 Closed Mon in winter 🚤 Vallaresso (San Marco)

Teamo (€)

This sleek, relaxing and modern wine bar makes a change from the traditional Venetian snack bar. There's a wide range of delicious *cicheti* at lunch, including both hot and cold fish or meat-based dishes, or try platters of mixed smoked meats and cheeses.

✉ Rio Terà della Mandola, San Marco 30124 ☎ 041 277 0850 🕐 Daily 8am–10pm 🚤 Sant'Angelo

Trattoria da Fiore (€€–€€€)

If you just want a quick bite, the *cicheti* here is excellent and can be eaten standing at the bar with a glass of wine among the locals. If you want more take a table and feast off *fritto misto* (mixed fried fish) or try the spaghetti with seafood.

✉ Calle delle Botteghe, San Marco 3461 ☎ 041 523 5310 🕐 Lunch, dinner. Closed Tue 🚤 San Samuele

Vini da Arturo (€€€)

This is one of the few restaurants in Venice to concentrate on meat dishes. In the pleasant wood-panelled dining room you'll find mainly locals dining on succulent steaks and veal.

🖂 Rio Terrà degli Assassini, San Marco 3656 ☎ 041 528 6974 🕓 Closed Sun 🚢 Sant'Angelo

SHOPPING

BEAUTY

Farmacia di Santa Novella

Step into this peaceful store and you'll be assailed by scent – from soaps, oils, essences, scents and candles. This is a branch of the famous Florentine pharmacy and all its products are hand-made using natural ingredients, all beautifully packaged.

🖂 Salizzada San Samuele, San Marco 3149 ☎ 041 522 0184
🚢 San Samuele

BOOKS AND PAPER

Libreria Mondadori

This big bookstore, one of Italy's top two chains, stocks a wide range of illustrated books on the city, guides and maps as well as a good selection of foreign-language publications.

🖂 Salizzada San Moisè, San Marco 1345 ☎ 041 522 2193;
www.libreriamondadorivenezia.it 🚢 Vallaresso (San Marco)

Libreria Studium

An excellent bookshop with a good range of maps, guidebooks and literature in English, including beautifully illustrated picture books and a children's range. They also stock English and other foreign novels.

🖂 Calle Canonica, San Marco 337/C ☎ 041 522 2382 🚢 San Zaccaria

Tassotti

Lovely paper and stationery store whose designs, unlike most paper in Venice, are based on flora and fauna; also imagery, old maps and prints. Choose from wrapping paper and bookmarks, post cards or greetings cards or splash out on desk accessories.

✉ Calle de la Bissa, San Marco 5471 ☎ 041 528 1881; www.tassotti.it
🚤 Rialto

FABRICS

Bevilacqua

This shop has an exquisite selection of both machine and handwoven fabrics, some made on original 17th-century looms. The Italian fashion houses, such as Dolce & Gabanna, come here for the wonderful velvets, taffetas, damasks, satins and brocades.
✉ Fondamenta della Canonica, San Marco 337/B ☎ 041 528 7581; www.luigi-bevilacqua.com 🚤 San Zaccaria

Gaggio

Some of the patterns in this shop are those once favoured by the designer and artist Mariano Fortuny (1871–1949), best remembered for the light, pleated silk dresses he produced. Wonderful hand-printed materials for a plethora of expensive products – cushions, bags, hats, dresses and more.
✉ Calle delle Botteghe, San Marco 3441–3451 ☎ 041 522 8574; www.gaggio.it 🚤 San Samuele

FASHION

Camicieria San Marco

Shirts and more shirts. Everything from top-brands to made to measure is here. Plus ties, pyjamas and bathrobes.
✉ Calle Vallaresso, San Marco 1340 ☎ 041 522 1432; www.shirtvenice.com 🚤 Vallaresso (San Marco)

Emporio Armani

As in every Italian city, this well-known fashion house is a good place to start exploring the chicest of clothes available.
✉ Calle dei Fabbri, San Marco 989; www.emporioarmani.com ☎ 041 523 7808 🚤 Rialto

Paul and Shark

A big name in men's casual wear, this is the place to come if you are looking for well-tailored, comfortable clothes and sportswear.

Their golf and yachting clothes are particularly popular.

✉ Mercerie, San Marco 4844 ☎ 041 523 7733 🚤 Rialto

GLASS

Pauly

This is one of the city's best outlets for Murano glass. The emphasis is on modern design, although there are some traditional pieces as well, plus some glass jewellery.

✉ Piazza San Marco 73 and 77, San Marco 4391A ☎ 041 520 9899; www.paulyglassfactory.com 🚤 Vallaresso (San Marco)

LEATHER GOODS AND SHOES

Bottega Veneta

Branches throughout the world. You can see the latest lines here first. Soft leathers for bags, belts, wallets and purses.

✉ Calle Vallaresso, San Marco 1337 ☎ 041 522 8489; www.bottegaveneta.com 🚤 Vallaresso (San Marco)

Calzature Casella

A Venetian institution and high in quality. Calzature Casella continues to bring out classic shoe designs but there will be variations every season, bringing tradition up to date.

✉ Campo San Salvador, San Marco 5048 ☎ 041 522 8848 🚤 Rialto

La Parigina

Located in the Mercerie shopping district. You can find all manner of well-known shoe brands and some lesser-known fun styles. Two well-known names include Clarks and Timberland. Look too for John Lobb and Vicini among the lesser-known makes. You can find another branch near the Scala di Bolovlo at San Marco 4336.

✉ Mercerie San Zulian, San Marco 727 ☎ 041 523 1555 🚤 Vallaresso (San Marco)

WOODWORK

Gianni Cavalier

Venetian craftsman producing painted and gilded furniture and frames for both pictures and mirrors – which make cheaper and more portable gifts. He still uses the centuries-old baroque designs and traditional gilding methods.

✉ Campo Santo Stefano, San Marco 2863/A ☎ 041 523 8621 🚊 Accademia

Livio de Marchi
It's not every day you see ordinary objects so beautifully carved in wood – a coat on a hanger, a pair of socks, a handbag or a hat. They are expensive but magnificent.

✉ Salizzada San Samuele, San Marco 3157/A ☎ 041 528 5694; www.liviodemarchi.com 🚊 San Samuele

ENTERTAINMENT

CLASSICAL MUSIC
Chiesa San Vidal
This 17th-century church is the permanent home of the Interpreti Veneziani, a chamber orchestra who give concerts throughout the year featuring the music of Vivaldi and his contemporaries.

✉ Campo San Vidal, San Marco 2862/B ☎ 041 277 0561; www.imusiciveneziani.com 🚊 Accademia

Santa Maria della Visitazione (La Pietà)
Vivaldi worshipped here and was the Master of Concerts. Today his work is celebrated along with other well-known composers, including Handel.

✉ Riva degli Schiavoni, San Marco ☎ 041 520 8767; www.pietavenezia.org 🚊 San Zaccaria

Scuola Grande di San Teodoro
A superb venue for the baroque and operatic concerts that are held from May to November.

✉ Salizzada San Teodoro, San Marco 4810 ☎ 041 521 0294; www.imusiciveneziani.com 🚊 Rialto

NIGHTLIFE
Bacaro Jazz
Mingle with the locals, and expect some gondoliers, at this popular nightspot. They serve a good range of cocktails and the

food is pretty good, too. But most people come here for the excellent jazz.

✉ Salizzida del Fontego dei Tedeschi, San Marco ☎ 041 528 5249 🕐 Daily Thu–Tue 4pm–3am 🚤 Rialto

Centrale

One of Venice's most fashionable bars, the super-hip Centrale is a restaurant and lounge with its own water entrance leading into a minimal and elegant space – open till late, a rarity in Venice.

✉ Piscina Frezzeriao, San Marco 1569 ☎ 041 296 0664 🚤 Vallaresso (San Marco)

Haig's Bar

Close to the Gritti Palace hotel (➤ 74), this American-style piano bar stays open late.

✉ Campo del Giglio, San Marco 5277 ☎ 041 528 9456 🕐 Daily 1:30–3, 7–2 🚤 Giglio

Vino Vino

Lovely place to enjoy a glass of wine (this is not the place for beer) in a bar that also serves food. Diverse crowd.

✉ Calle delle Veste, San Marco 2007/A ☎ 041 241 7688 🕐 Wed–Mon 10.30am–midnight 🚤 Vallaresso (San Marco)

OPERA, BALLET AND THEATRE

Teatro Carlo Goldoni

Venice's principal venue for Italian and international drama, mostly performed in Italian, is named after Venice's greatest playwright. Also hosts some pop concerts usually featuring Italian artists.

✉ Calle Goldini, San Marco 4650/B ☎ 041 240 2011 🚤 Rialto

Teatro La Fenice

La Fenice (➤ 89) is primarily an opera house but also stages ballet and concerts. Reservations for tickets are essential; obtain in advance from the box office, by telephone or on the internet.

✉ Campo San Fantin, San Marco 1965; www.teatrolafenice.it ☎ 041 2424 (call centre) 🚤 Giglio

Castello

Castello is the most easterly of Venice's six *sestieri*, and one whose many quiet corners, delightful churches and other sights are often overlooked by visitors seduced by the more immediate attractions of nearby San Marco.

CASTELLO

Walk to its eastern margins, beyond the Arsenale, Venice's vast former shipyards, and you'll find a very different city, one with few visitors and plenty of working Venetians. Even close to San Marco, in squares around the fine church of San Giovanni in Bragora, or the more distant San Francesco della Vigna, little neighbourhood bars and shops lend the district a different air. Be sure to wander at random, but also to see gems such as Santi Giovanni e Paolo and the Scuola di San Giorgio degli Schiavoni.

ARSENALE

The naval powerhouse of the Venetian Empire was the Arsenale, the great dockyard in the east of the city. Surrounded by 15th-century castellated walls and entered through a monumental archway and watergate, it was where the galleys that conquered the Mediterranean and dominated it for centuries were built and based. The interior, used as an exhibition space during the Biennale, is now mostly deserted dockside and bare walls, but the gates – guarded by stone lions brought from Greece in the 17th and 18th centuries – can easily be admired from the *campo* (square) outside.

✚ 24J ✉ Campiello della Malvasia ✋ Moderate
🚢 Arsenale

CAMPO SANTI GIOVANNI E PAOLO

On the San Marco side of the Grand Canal, this square in front of the huge church of Santi Giovanni e Paolo (➤ 48–49) is dominated by the remarkable equestrian bronze statue of Bartolomeo Colleoni, a famous Venetian general of the 15th century.

✚ 10F 🚢 Fondamenta Nove/Ospedale

CAMPO SANTA MARIA FORMOSA

Campo Santa Maria Formosa, around the church of that name (➤ 109), is busy with market stalls and open-air café tables.

✚ 21G 🚢 San Zaccaria/Rialto

GIARDINI PUBBLICI

On the city's eastern fringes in Castello, this garden is a welcome green space after a heavy dose of architectural grandeur. It was created by Napoleon,

who oversaw the draining of a stretch of marshland and the demolition of several convents to generate this shady haven. It is good for a break from the crowds and pleasant for a picnic. You may notice the pavilions partly hidden by the trees. Used in the Biennale, the biennial art and film exhibition held from June to September (➤ 25), these are closed to the public except during the event. The rest is a grassy space dotted with benches, with wide views over the lagoon.

🚹 24K (off map) 👪 Free 🚢 Giardini

MUSEO DIOCESANO D'ARTE SACRA

This extraordinary museum is a store-room and restoration centre for works of art from local churches and monasteries. Some are stolen pieces that have been retrieved by the police. It makes for an interesting display of sculpture, silverware and other work, with changing exhibitions in the upstairs gallery. The building dates from the 12th to 13th centuries, but the museum's main draw is its Romanesque cloister, once the focal point of the Benedictine monastery of Sant'Apollonia, the only cloister of this period in the city and a gloriously tranquil place to visit.

www.museodiocesanovenezia.it

🚹 21J ✉ Sant'Apollonia, Castello 4312 ☎ 041 277 1702 🕐 Daily 10–6 👪 Expensive 🚢 San Zaccaria

MUSEO DELLA FONDAZIONE QUERINI STAMPALIA

The Querini Stampalia *palazzo* was the home of another grand Venetian family and 20 rooms are still furnished with their splendid collection of pictures and furniture, accumulated by aristocrat Giovanni Querini in the 19th century. His foundation specified the opening of a library to promote learning, and it is still used enthusiastically by students today.
www.querinistampalia.it

✚ 21H ✉ Campiello Querini Stampalia, Castello 5252 ☎ 041 523 4411
🕐 Tue–Sat 10–8, Sun 10–7 ⚫ Moderate 🚤 San Zaccaria

MUSEO STORICO NAVALE

The Naval Museum records the illustrious maritime past of Venice with a magnificent collection of ship models, pictures and relics housed in an old granary near the Arsenale (➤ 102), which was the naval base of the Republic. The exhibits range from models of the galleys that fought the corsairs and Turks to the human torpedoes used in World War II. There is a special section devoted entirely to the gondola and other Venetian craft, with actual boats displayed in part of the Arsenale itself.

✚ 24K ✉ Campo San Biagio, Castello 2148 ☎ 041 520 0276 🕐 Mon–Fri 8:45–1:30, Sat 8:45–1 ⚫ Inexpensive 🚤 Arsenale

RIVA DEGLI SCHIAVONI

The Riva degli Schiavoni, or 'The Waterfront of the Slavs', is the principal waterside promenade of Venice, running eastwards from the Doges' Palace to the Ca' di Dio canal, where its name changes and then continuing to the Giardini (public gardens). After the Doges' Palace and the adjoining State Prison comes the Danieli (➤ 74) and a succession of other grand hotels facing the Basin of San Marco. The wide, paved Riva, broken by a succession of

bridges over canals, is cluttered with café tables and souvenir-sellers' stalls at its western end, while its waterside is busy with *vaporetto* piers and the pleasure boats and tugs that moor there. Leading from the Riva to the north are many alleys and archways running into the maze of the city and to a few squares, notably the Campo San Zaccaria and the Campo Bandiera e Moro.

✚ 22J 🚤 San Zaccaria

SAN FRANCESCO DELLA VIGNA

This superb Palladian church, one of Venice's best kept secrets, is in the less-visited northeast of the city close to the Arsenale, and its huge campanile is sometimes mistaken for that of San Marco from a distance. It contains beautiful paintings – although none of the first rank – including a delightful 15th-century *Madonna and Child Enthroned* by Antonio da Negroponte, plus a serene cloister.

✚ 24G ✉ Campo di San Francesco, Castello 2786 ☎ 041 520 6102
🕐 Daily 8–12, 3–7 💷 Free 🚤 Ospedale/Celestia

a walk to the gardens of Castello

Start at the Palazzo Ducale on the edge of San Marco and turn left onto Riva degli Schiavoni. As you go over the first bridge look to the left to see the renowned Ponte dei Sospiri (Bridge of Sighs). Continuing along you can see the famous Danieli hotel – named after its first proprietor Dal Niel – before crossing the next bridge. Housed in a former 15th-century *palazzo* it has been a hotel since the early 19th century, its interior retaining many of the original features. At this point out across the water is the Isola di San Giorgio Maggiore, with its striking church (➤ 46–47).

Carry on along the waterfront, pausing to look back over your shoulder at the superb view. Go over the next bridge and pass the church of La Pietà (➤ 109). Continue over two more bridges and go past the Arsenale vaporetto stop and over the next bridge into Campo San Biagio with the Museo Storico Navale (➤ 104). Continue along Riva dei Sette Martiri as far as the Giardini Pubblici (➤ 102–103). After the Giardini vaporetto stop turn left into the gardens where you will see the Biennale Internazionale d'Arte in front of you. Turn left and keep bearing left until first right takes you into Viale Garibaldi with the Garibaldi monument at the end. Go through the impressive gates at the end and turn left into Via Giuseppe Garibaldi.

This vibrant street is in the heart of working-class Castello, where you will feel a long way from the popular narrow streets and canals of the tourist trail.

About 150m (163yds) on the right take the narrow alley Calle del Forno, crossing the bridge at the end. Turn left and at the canal turn right to the Arsenale (▶ 102). Cross the bridge and keep on to the church of San Martino (▶ 110). Go around the church and continue with the canal on your right until you reach Calle della Pegola. Turn down here and at the end turn right into Calle dei Forni, which takes you back to the waterfront. The Arsenale vaporetto stop is almost right in front of you.

Distance 3.5km (2 miles)
Time 2 hours plus stops
Start point Palazzo Ducale ✚ 21J
End point Arsenale *vaporetto* stop ✚ 23J
Lunch Take a refreshment stop among the locals at Via Giuseppe Garibaldi

SAN GIORGIO DEI GRECI

The church is quickly recognizable by its dangerously tilted 16th-century campanile, caused by gradual subsidence. The church of the Greek community, many of whom were refugees from Constantinople when it was taken by the Turks in the 15th century, has strong Byzantine and Greek Orthodox decoration.

✚ 22H ✉ Fondamenta dei Greci, Castello 3412 ☎ 041 523 9569
🕐 Wed–Mon 9–11, 2:30–4:30 ✋ Free 🚢 San Zaccaria

SAN GIOVANNI IN BRAGORA

This fascinating little parish church, where Antonio Vivaldi was baptized, lies hidden in a quiet campo off the Riva degli Schiavoni, and a plaque outside records the date of the baptism as 6 May, 1678. Among the paintings in the church is a lovely, peaceful

Madonna and Child with Saints by Bartolomeo Vivarini. Over the high altar there is another highlight, the painting of the *Baptism of Christ* (1492) by Cima da Conegliano.

✚ 23J ✉ Campo Bandiera e Moro, Castello 2464 ☎ 041 520 5906
🕙 Mon–Sat 9–11, 3:30–5:30 ✋ Free 🚤 Arsenale

SANTI GIOVANNI E PAOLO
Best places to see, pages 48–49.

SANTA MARIA FORMOSA

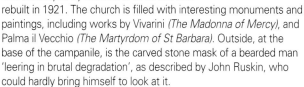

The 15th-century church dominates a large square enlivened by cafés and market stalls. Designed by Mauro Codussi in 1492, it was revamped according to Renaissance ideals while retaining its original Byzantine plan. The dome was destroyed by a bomb in 1916 but was rebuilt in 1921. The church is filled with interesting monuments and paintings, including works by Vivarini *(The Madonna of Mercy)*, and Palma il Vecchio *(The Martyrdom of St Barbara)*. Outside, at the base of the campanile, is the carved stone mask of a bearded man 'leering in brutal degradation', as described by John Ruskin, who could hardly bring himself to look at it.

✚ 21G ✉ Campo Santa Maria Formosa, Castello 5263 ☎ 041 523 4645, 041 275 0462 🕙 Mon–Sat 10–5, Sun 1–5 ✋ Inexpensive 🚤 San Zaccaria

SANTA MARIA DELLA VISITAZIONE (LA PIETÀ)
This has been used for concerts since the 17th century, and during the 18th century Vivaldi composed music for the choir. Music is still played here regularly, when audiences can admire the oval painting by Giambattista Tiepolo on the ceiling, *The Coronation of the Virgin*. The church is only opened for concerts.
www.vivaldi.it

✚ 22J ✉ Riva degli Schiavoni, Castello ☎ 041 523 1096 🕙 Varies for concerts ✋ Varies for concerts 🚤 San Zaccaria

SAN MARTINO

This is a lovely, little-visited church near the Arsenale, and it is probable that the wooden angels and cherubs around the organ were carved by craftsmen who decorated the great galleys in the dockyard. It has another spectacular ceiling painted with an *Ascension into Heaven*, past the pillars of an atrium, that seems to grow out of the architecture. The profusion of monuments and paintings makes this a very Venetian church, and outside in the wall is one of the now rare 'lion's mask' letter boxes (mailboxes) for notes that decounce enemies of the state.

➕ 24J 🖂 Campo San Martino, Castello 2298 🕑 Irregular hours 💵 Free 🚤 Arsenale

SAN PIETRO DI CASTELLO

As it stands forlornly on its little island at the far eastern extremity of Venice, the church seems to be dreaming of past glories. This was the first of the central Venetian islands to be settled, and the church became the cathedral of Venice in AD775, remaining so until 1807, when the Basilica di San Marco, formerly the Doges' private chapel, took its place. Its isolation here throughout the life of the Venetian Republic was a deliberate attempt to minimize the influence of the Pope and Rome. It overlooks a usually deserted stretch of grass and trees. Inside, the church, which was built to a Palladian design in the 16th century, is lofty and rather grand but, above all, neglected.

➕ 24K (off map) 🖂 Campo San Pietro, Castello 70, Isola di San Pietro ☎ 041 523 8950 🕑 Mon–Sat 10–5 💵 Inexpensive 🚤 Giardini

SAN ZACCARIA

The massive 16th-century church – with traces of its predecessors – is filled with paintings. The most celebrated of these is Bellini's *Madonna and Four Saints* (1505) in the second chapel on the left. During the Venetian Republic, the nunnery attached to the church was favoured by rich families as a refuge for their unattached

daughters. There is also a permanently waterlogged crypt where eight early doges are interred.

✚ 22J ✉ Campo San Zaccaria, Castello 4963 ☎ 041 522 1257 🕐 Mon–Sat 10–12, 4–6, Sun 11–12, 4–6 ✋ Free; inexpensive to chapels, sacristy and crypt 🚢 San Zaccaria

SCUOLA GRANDE DI SAN MARCO

Another magnificent *scuola* with a fine exterior stands next to the church of Santi Giovanni e Paolo and now houses the main hospital; visited by appointment only. Its most interesting works of art, relief carvings incoporating startling perspectives, can be seen on the outside wall facing the campo.

✚ 10E ✉ San Giovanni e Paolo, Castello 🚢 Ospedale Civile

SCUOLA DI SAN GIORGIO DEGLI SCHIAVONI

This tiny, initimate building was set up in 1451 to look after the interests of Venice's Dalmatian, or Slav, population, formerly slaves but by the 15th century established as merchants and sailors. The *scuola* houses the early 16th-century Vittore Carpaccio's paintings as its main attraction, an enchanting frieze illustrating the lives of three Dalmatian saints: St George, St Jerome and St Tryphon. This cycle of paintings can be found on the upper part of the walls in the ground floor hall. Ranged below one of the most lavish of ceilings, the cycle begins with the story of *St George Slaying the Dragon*, an exceptionally graphic and detailed painting, followed by the *Triumph of St George, St George Baptising the Gentiles* and the *Miracle of St Tryphon*. The next two, the *Agony in the Garden* and the *Calling of St Matthew*, precede three works concerning the life of St Jerome, the best-loved being *St Augustine in his Study* at the moment of Jerome's death – an intimate glimpse into a medieval Venetian study, complete with appealing dog.

➕ 23H ✉ Calle Furlani, Castello 3259A ☎ 041 522 8828 🕙 Mon 2:45–6, Tue–Sat 9:15–1, 2:45–6, Sun 9:15–1 ✋ Inexpensive 🚤 San Zaccaria/Arsenale

HOTELS

Danieli (€€€€)
See page 74.

Foresteria Valdese (€€)
This is a hostel with a difference. Housed in the magnifiecent Palazzo Cavagnis near the lively Campo Santa Maria Formosa, it is run by the Waldensian and Methodist church in Venice. Accommodation ranges from dormitory beds (only available for groups by reservation) to comfortable doubles (75 beds in total).
✉ Calle della Madonetta, Castello 5170 ☎ 041 528 6797; www.diaconivaldese.org/venezia/foresteria 🚣 Rialto

La Residenza (€–€€)
This intensely Venetian *pensione* has a magnificent salon with paintings, plasterwork and chandeliers. Passages lead from the salon to the 15 comfortable bedrooms.
✉ Bandiera e Moro, Castello 3608 ☎ 041 528 315; www.venicelaresidenza.com 🚣 Arsenale

Londra Palace (€€€–€€€€)
See page 75.

Metropole (€€€)
Another hotel on the Riva degli Schiavoni with a fine view of the Basin of San Marco. The 70 spacious rooms are nicely decorated with paintings and furnished with anitques and period furniture.
✉ Riva degli Schiavoni, Castello 4199 ☎ 041 520 5044; www.hotelmetropole.com 🚣 Vallaresso (San Marco)

Scandinavia (€€€)
Located in one of Venice's nicest squares, this hotel is comfortable and spacious, with the furnishings reflecting the 18th century. The 37 rooms are well equipped but be aware that the prices go up for those overlooking the square.
✉ Campo Santa Maria Formosa, Castello 5240 ☎ 041 522 3507; www.scandinaviahotel.com 🚣 Rialto

RESTAURANTS

Ai Corazzieri (€–€€)
See page 58.

Al Covo (€€€)
Seriously devoted to fish. Be guided by the waiter to get the best out of this experience. Only the best ingredients are used in creating the traditional Venetian recipes. Be sure to reserve ahead.
✉ Campiello della Pescaria, Castello 3968 ☎ 041 522 3812 🕐 Lunch, dinner. Closed Wed, Thu 🚤 Arsenale

Alle Testiere (€€€)
It may be small but its reputation is huge. Imaginative cooking using local fish blended with delicious spices and herbs.
✉ Calle del Mondo Novo, Castello 5801 ☎ 041 522 7220 🕐 Lunch, dinner (two dinner sittings). Closed Sun, Mon and Aug 🚤 Rialto

Al Mascaron (€–€€)
Down to earth bar-cum-trattoria with snacks such as the tapas-like *cicheti* but also a menu with pasta, risotto, fish and seafood and salads as well. It's best to reserve.
✉ Calle Lunga Santa Maria Formosa, Castello 5225 ☎ 041 522 5995
🕐 Lunch, dinner. Closed Sun 🚤 San Zaccaria

Corte Sconta (€€€)
This popular Venetian restaurant is always busy. It's also off the main tourist drag and the cooking is first rate. Although particularly noted for its fresh fish and seafood classics, the pastas and traditional desserts are also excellent.
✉ Calle di Pestrin, Castello 3886 ☎ 041 522 7024 🕐 Lunch, dinner. Closed Jan to early Feb, mid-Jul to mid-Aug 🚤 Arsenale

Dal Pampo/Osteria Sant'Elena (€€)
Good wholesome cooking and full bodied wines. Primarily a local's place but you will be made very welcome.
✉ Calle Generale Chinotto, Castello 24 ☎ 041 520 8419 🕐 Lunch, dinner. Closed Wed and 1 week in May and Aug 🚤 Sant'Elena

Da Remigio (€€)

One of the more authentic trattoria and as a result popular, so reserve a table. Excellent antipasti and the freshest of fish.

✉ Salizzada dei Greci, Castello 3416 ☎ 041 523 0089 🕐 Lunch, dinner. Closed Mon dinner, Tue, Jan and 2 weeks during Jul or Aug 🚤 San Zaccaria

Osteria Oliva Nera (€€€)

Venetian classics meet modern cooking. Dishes include succulent lamb cooked in thyme, octopus salad and tempting desserts. An offshoot restaurant, Oliva Nera II, has opened at 3446 in the same street (closed Thu).

✉ Salizzada dei Greci, Castello 3417/18 ☎ 041 522 2170 🕐 Lunch, dinner. Closed Wed 🚤 San Zaccaria

SHOPPING

ACCESSORIES AND MASKS

Arabesque Barbieri

Off the beaten track, this elegant and tempting store sell nothing but scarves, stoles and pashminas in beautiful fabrics and colours, ranging from cashmere and feather-light wool, to chunky thick felts and gossamer silks.

✉ Ponte dei Greci, Castello 3403 ☎ 041 522 8177 🚤 San Zaccaria

Papier Mâché

If you're looking for a mask and want something more original and contemporary, this is the place to come for beautiful and authentically made one-off designs. They may not be inexpensive, but they are real heirlooms.

✉ Calle Lunga Santa Maria Formosa, Castello 5175 ☎ 041 522 9995 🚤 Rialto/San Zaccaria

FASHION

Mistero

Two shops next door to each other: young fashion, ladies' clothes (including larger sizes) and homeware. Atelier, selling the women's clothes, has some lovely items imported from India.

✉ Ruga Giuffa, Castello 4755 ☎ 041 522 7797 🚤 San Zaccaria

HOMEWARE
Ratti
Venice's top hardware and kitchen store rambles over a big space and sells everything from potato peelers and light bulbs to seriously covetable Italian china and kitchenware.

✉ Calle delle Bande, Castello 5825 ☎ 041 240 4600 🚊 Rialto/San Zaccaria

Resmini Passamanerie
Venetian traditional style is rich in decorative touches such as trimmings, braids and tassels, and you'll find an excellent selection at this traditional shop as well as wools and haberdashery trimmings galore.

✉ Salizzada San Lio, Castello 5784 ☎ 041 523 5141 🚊 Rialto/San Zaccaria

JEWELLERY
Anticlea Antiquariato
One of the best in the city for antique glass beads, the shop is stuffed full with every colour and style. They will make up necklaces, braclets or earrings for you or you can buy ready-made.

✉ Calle San Provolo, Castello 4719/A ☎ 041 528 6946 🚊 San Zaccaria

TOYS
Lanterna Magica
This is Venice's best traditional toyshop, which specializes in educational and exciting toys and games for all ages from all over the world, as well as delightful teddy bears by Steiff and beautiful porcelain dolls.

✉ Calle delle Bande, Castello 5379 ☎ 041 528 1902 🚊 Rialto/San Zaccaria

ENTERTAINMENT

NIGHTLIFE
Inishark
It may be another Irish pub abroad but it's a nice one and you get a very warm welcome from the Italian owners. Guinness to drink and football (soccer) on the wide-screen TV.

✉ Calle del Mondo Novo, Castello 5787 ☎ 041 523 5300 🕐 Tue–Sun 6pm–1:30am 🚊 Rialto

CANNAREGIO

Cannaregio

Most visitors have only a fleeting acquaintance with Cannaregio, the *sestiere* that embraces much of northern Venice, passing swiftly through it as they walk or take a boat from the railway station to Piazza San Marco. Yet its many quiet corners and distinctive areas, such as the old Jewish ghetto, are some of Venice's most seductive and unvisited.

Here, as in Castello, you are often a long way from the hordes, but – as ever in Venice – only moments from beautiful buildings, pretty squares and sudden, unexpected views. Madonna dell'Orto is the loveliest church and the Ca' d'Oro the most tempting museum, but don't overlook the old ghetto's fascinating Museo Ebraico or the tucked-away churches of San Giobbe and Sant'Alvise.

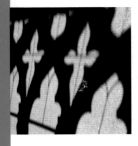

CA' D'ORO

The 'House of Gold', the most famous *palazzo* on the Grand Canal, was named after the gilding on its elaborate exterior when it was new. Inside the *palazzo* an elegant new gallery displays Italian art, including frescoes by Titian and Giorgione. Reopened in 1984, this magnificent building retains its architectural bones, but sadly not its atmosphere of former grandeur. You can get a really good view of the *palazzo* from the opposite side of the Grand Canal at the Pescheria (fish market). **www.**cadoro.org

➕ 7E ✉ Calle di Ca' d'Oro, Cannaregio 3932 ☎ 041 520 0345 ⏰ Mon 8:15–2, Tue–Sun 8:15–7:15 ✋ Moderate 🚤 Ca' d'Oro

CAMPO DEI MORI

This oddly shaped little campo, tucked away near the northern waterfront, gets its name from the four 14th-century statues of turbaned moors (*mori*) ranged round its sides. The one on the corner, who sports a replacement iron nose, was nicknamed Sior Antonio Rioba by the Venetians and was once used as a place to leave denunciatory letters destined for the powers-that-be. Round the corner on the canal, number 3399 was the artist Titian's house.

➕ 7B 🚤 Orto

GESUITI (SANTA MARIA ASSUNTA)

The early 18th-century Jesuits built their church to impress, and the statuary along the skyline of its pediment gives a hint of what is within. Inside, the pillars and floor seem to be hung with green and white damask silk, which is also draped around the pulpit on the north wall, but it all turns out to be marble.

➕ 9D ✉ Campo dei Gesuiti, Cannaregio 4885 ☎ 041 528 6579 ⏰ Daily 10–12, 3–6 ✋ Free 🚤 Fondamenta Nove

IL GHETTO

This a small district enclosed by canals in the northwest of the city and not far from the rail station. It was named after a 14th-century cannon-casting foundry, or *geto* in Venetian – the name was subsequently given to Jewish enclaves the world over. Since Jews were only permitted to live in this small area from 1516 to 1797, they were allowed to build higher houses than elsewhere in the city and so the buildings rise to eight floors.

The main approach to the Ghetto is through a narrow alley leading off the Fondamenta di Cannaregio. This brings you to the Ghetto Vecchio and over a bridge to the Campo Ghetto Nuovo, a separate island that's the heart of the Ghetto and where you will find the Holocaust Memorial, a series of seven reliefs by Arbit Blatas, commemorating the deportation and extermination of the city's Jews, and the **Museo Ebraico.** The museum opened in 1955 and displays a collection of religious objects, prayer books, textiles, documents and silverware.

Today the area remains the focus for the religion, and there are still a small number of Jewish families living in the Ghetto, with two synagogues in regular use.

www.ghetto.it; **www.**museoebraico.it

✚ 4C 🛥 Guglie

Museo Ebraico

✉ Campo del Ghetto Nuovo 2902B ☎ 041 715 359
🕐 Jun–Sep Sun–Fri 10–7; Oct–May 10–5:30. May close early on Fri ✋ Moderate

MADONNA DELL'ORTO

Isolated in the north of the city in Cannaregio, the church is a good goal for a long walk. It was magnificently restored after the flood of 1966 by funds raised in Britain. Spend a few minutes to admire the mainly Gothic façade before entering the church. The windows are obviously Gothic, the onion-shaped dome echoes the earlier Byzantine style, while the elegant doorway is clearly Renaissance.

The simple interior, with its sense of space, height and light, is laid out in basilica form. Tintoretto, who is buried in one of the side chapels – you can see his tomb – was a parishioner and painted some superb pictures as a gift to the church. In the chancel are the magnificent *Last Judgement* and *The Making of the Golden Calf*. Look for the charming *Presentation of the Virgin* at the end of the right nave above the door. In the apse there are further paintings by Tintoretto, the *Beheading of St Paul* and *St Peter's Vision of the Cross*, full of movement and pathos. Other great works include Cima da Conegliano's *St John the Baptist*.

The church gained its name from the story of a statue of the Madonna and Child found in a local vegetable garden or *orto*, and believed to have worked miracles. The statue is in the Cappella di San Mauro off the end of the right aisle near the main altar.

➕ 7B ✉ Campo della Madonna dell'Orto, Cannaregio 3520 ☎ 041 719 933 🕓 Mon–Sat 10–5 💰 Inexpensive 🚤 Orto

PALAZZO LABIA

Palazzo Labia, not far from the Santa Lucia rail station, is now the headquarters of the Italian broadcasting service, RAI. It contains one of the loveliest rooms in Venice, decorated by the elder Tiepolo with gloriously coloured frescoes of Antony and Cleopatra in 16th-century dress and dramatic perspectives.

➕ 4D ✉ Campo San Geremia ☎ 041 524 2812, 041 781 277 🕓 Call for latest hours 💰 Call to inquire 🚤 Guglie

SANT'ALVISE

Although one of the most remote churches in the city, this is a useful destination for a long walk including the Madonna dell'Orto (➤ opposite) and the Ghetto (➤ 119). The façade is pure Gothic, while inside the church retains little of its original single-nave, basilical form and now incorporates Venice's first example of hanging choir, installed in the 15th century. Firstly admire the charming 17th-century trompe-l'oeil ceiling, three stunning canvases by Giambattista Tiepolo (1696–1770).

➕ 6A ✉ Campo Sant'Alvise, Cannaregio ☎ 041 524 4664, 041 275 0462 🕙 Mon–Sat 10–5 ✋ Inexpensive 🚏 Sant'Alvise

SANTI APOSTOLI

There has been a church on this site since the 9th century, and the present 16th-century church incorporates some parts of the early building, with the interior reflecting some 18th-century additions. The church is worth visiting just for *The Communion of Santa Lucia* by the elder Tiepolo in the delightful 15th-century Corner family chapel. The exceptionally tall 17th-century campanile, crowned by an onion dome, is a well-known Venetian landmark.

➕ 8E ✉ Campo dei Santi Apostoli, Cannaregio 4542 ☎ 041 523 8297 🕙 Mon–Sat 7:30–11:30, 5–7, Sun 8:30–12, 4.15–6:30 ✋ Free 🚏 Ca' d'Oro

SAN GEREMIA E LUCIA

Standing on the corner of the Grand Canal and the Canale di Cannaregio, this vast, light, plain church, originally dedicated solely to St Jerome, is now remarkable for housing the mummified body of St Lucia, which was removed from her own church when it was demolished to make way for the rail station that was to be named after her. Wearing a gold mask and a red and gold robe, she lies in a glass case.

✚ 4D ✉ Campo San Geremia, Cannaregio 334 🕓 Mon–Fri 8:30–12, 3:30–6:30, Sun 9:30–12, 5:30–6:30 ✋ Free 🚤 San Marcuola/Ferrovia

SAN GIOBBE

Distinctly Florentine in design, San Giobbe is dedicated to the Old Testament figure Job, and was built around 1463 following a Venetian visit by the fiery Tuscan preacher, San Bernardino of Siena. The interior is pure Renaissance and is notable for the polychrome terracotta works by the Florentine della Robbia family, found in the Cappella Martini. The doorway and chancel are the work of the Lombardo family, as is much of the church's sculpture.

✚ 2B ✉ Campo San Giobbe, Cannaregio 620 ☎ 041 524 1889 🕓 Mon–Sat 10–5 ✋ Inexpensive 🚤 Ponte dei Tre Archi

SAN GIOVANNI CRISOSTOMO

Just a few minutes' walk north from the Rialto is San Giovanni Crisostomo, literally St John the Golden-Tongued, a small, busy, Venetian parish church and an excellent example of Renaissance architecture. Its architect, the Renaissance master Mauro Codussi, based his design around the Greek cross form. Richly decorated, it is remarkable for a lovely painting showing *Saints Jerome, Christopher and Louis of Toulouse* by Giovanni Bellini.

✚ 8F ✉ Campo San Giovanni Crisostomo, Cannaregio 5889 ☎ 041 522 7155 🕐 Mon–Sat 8:30–12, 3:30–5, Sun 3:30–5:30 ✋ Free 🚤 Rialto

SANTA MARIA DEI MIRACOLI

One of the most exquisite small buildings in Venice, this church has often been described as looking like a jewel box. Built in the 15th century of softly coloured marble, it stands beside a canal with such elegance that its design needs no embellishment to satisfy the eye. Have a good look around the outside before

venturing inside. The church was built to house an image of the Virgin painted in 1409 by Nicolò di Pietro, which had been placed in a street shrine. The image became exceedingly popular and credited with miraculous powers, and Pietro Lombardo was commissioned to build the church, a Renaissance triumph.

Inside, the marble theme continues in brilliant tones, with some of the most wonderfully intricate carving to be found in any church in the city. Lombardo and his sons, Tullio and Antonio, executed an array of beautifully sculpted saints leading to the raised choir. Look up to admire the striking ceiling, covered with 50 *Saints and Prophets* (1528) by Pier Pennacchi. The church is understandably a popular wedding venue.

✚ 9E 🕐 Campo dei Miracoli, Cannaregio 6075 ☎ 041 275 0462 🕐 Mon–Sat 10–5 ✋ Inexpensive 🚤 Ca' d'Oro/Rialto

SCALZI (SANTA MARIA DI NAZARETTA)

Close to the rail station, the church is well placed for those
wanting a first, or last, look at something intensely Venetian. The
scalzi were 'barefooted' Carmelite friars who came here in the
mid-17th century and commissioned the church. The ornate
baroque façade is an indication of the sumptuous but gloomy
interior of multi-coloured marble, statuary and 18th-century
paintings. Appropriately, the last of the doges, Ludovico Manin,
is buried there.

🔁 3D ✉ Fondamenta Scalzi, Cannaregio ☎ 041 715 115 🕐 Daily 8–12:50,
4–6:50 🚶 Free 🚃 Ferrovia

HOTELS

Giorgione (€€€)

Based in a 15th-century *palazzo* and a newer building, the 76 rooms are decorated in period style, all with great attention to detail. There is a flower-filled courtyard, complete with lily pond, for taking breakfast.

✉ Campo Santi Apostoli, Cannaregio 4587 ☎ 041 522 5810; www.hotelgiorgione.com 🚤 Ca' d'Oro

Rossi (€)

Great for budget accommodation, the Rossi has excellent rates throughout the year. Rooms, some with shared bathrooms, are clean, simple and modern and it's well situated on the Lista di Spagna, the main drag heading east from the station.

✉ Lista di Spagna, Cannaregio 262 ☎ 041 715 164; www.hotelrossi.ve.net 🚤 Ferrovia

RESTAURANTS

Al Bacco (€€)

See page 58.

Algiubagio (€)

Conveniently placed when waiting for the boat at Fondamente Nuove, plus views of the cemetery at San Michele. Mingle with the locals for a quick bite – breakfast, pizza and some nice ice cream.

✉ Fondamente Nuove, Cannaregio 5039 ☎ 041 523 6084
🕐 Breakfast–8:30pm. Closed Tue 🚤 Fondamente Nuove

Antica Mola (€€€)

Nice setting for a warm night sitting beside the canal or in the garden at the back. Fresh fish of the day and whatever else the chef fancies creating.

✉ Fondamenta dei Ormesini, Cannaregio 2800 ☎ 041 717 492 🕐 Lunch, dinner. Closed Wed and Aug 🚤 San Marcuola

Fiaschetteria Toscana (€€€)

Established in 1956 and despite the name the menu includes

classic Venetian dishes and excellent seafood, all lovingly prepared. Great selection of wines from Tuscany.

✉ Salizzada San Giovanni Grisostomo, Cannaregio 5719 ☎ 041 528 5281
🕐 Lunch, dinner. Closed Mon dinner, Tue and 3 weeks in Jul 🚢 Rialto

Osteria Al Bomba (€€)

Popular with gondoliers for its good value and tasty snacks. Although main dishes are usually of fish, this restaurant is a good bet for vegetarians, with a selection cooked in imaginative ways. Look beyond the rather plain surroundings and it's worth the visit.

✉ Calle del Oca, Cannaregio 4297/98 ☎ 041 520 5175 🕐 Lunch, dinner
🚢 Ca' d'oro

Osteria Da Rioba (€€–€€€)

Popular among the younger Venetian set, this restaurant is named after the Moorish statue in the nearby Palazzo Mastelli. Minimalist in comparison to the usual *osteria*, its emphasis is on Venetian classics, such as rabbit stew and fish dishes.

✉ Fondamenta della Misericordia, Cannaregio 2553 ☎ 041 524 4379
🕐 Lunch, dinner. Closed Mon 🚢 Madonna dell'Orto

Vini da Gigio (€€)

The perfect setting for an atmospheric dinner, in two intimate, rustic dining rooms by the canal. This is the one for an authentic and traditional home-cooked Venetian meal. The menu is seafood based but meat and game also feature.

✉ Fondamenta San Felice, Cannaregio 3628A ☎ 041 528 5140 🕐 Lunch, dinner. Closed Mon, Tue and 3 weeks in Aug 🚢 Ca' d'Oro

SHOPPING
DEPARTMENT STORE
Coin

Probably the most popular, and certainly one of the best, of Italy's chain department stores. A full wardrobe, plus accessories, available at good prices, and you can also buy linen and homewares.

✉ Salizzada San Crisostomo, Cannaregio 5787 ☎ 041 520 3581 🚢 Rialto

HOMEWARE
TSL

This is Venice's best mid-market household linen store and carries a wonderful selection of towels, bathroom textiles, bed linen and quilts as well as dressing gowns for men and women. The wide range is at an equally good range of prices. There's another branch at the Rialto.

✉ Strada Nuova, Cannaregio, 1318 ☎ 041 718 524 🚤 Ca d'Or

MEN'S FASHION
Camicissima

There are bargain prices here on men's shirts, beautifully tailored in pure cotton and poplin. Italian style in a huge range of fabric designs and colours – buy two and get one practically free.

✉ Rio Terra della Maddalena, Cannaregio 1367 ☎ 041 275 0925
🚤 San Marcuola

ENTERTAINMENT

CONTEMPORARY DANCE
Teatro Fondamente Nuove

Located in an old carpenter's shop, this is Venice's foremost avant-garde venue. Works staged include contemporary dance, workshops and exhibitions as well as film festivals and innovative arts projects.

✉ Fondamente Nuove, Cannaregio 5013 ☎ 041 522 4498
🚤 Fondamente Nuove

NIGHTLIFE
Casinò Municipale

On the Canal Grande in the opulent Palazzo Vendramin-Calergi, the Casinó offers roulette, baccarat and blackjack, as well as slot machines and electronic games. You will have to dress up – jacket and tie for men.

✉ Palazzo Vendramin Calergi, Calle Largo Vendramin, of Rio Terrà della Maddalena, Cannaregio 2040 ☎ 041 529 7111; www.casinovenezia.it
🕐 Daily 2:45pm–2:30am (slot machines daily 3:30pm–2:30am)
🚤 San Marcuola

Iguana

If sangria, burritos, fajitas and singing is your thing, this Mexican bar/restaurant is just the place to let your hair down. Arrive later rather than earlier.

✉ Fondmenta della Misericordia, Canneregio 2515 ☎ 041 713 561

🕐 Tue–Sun 6pm–2am 🚤 Madonna dell'Orto

Paradiso Perduto

Venice's favourite and longest-established nightspot is one of a string along the Fondamenta della Misericordia – the city's hottest spot for young Venetians. Themed parties, cheap food and drink and a buzzing atmosphere continue to pull in the crowds. You'll be guaranteed a good night out.

✉ Fondamenta della Misericordia, Cannaregio 2640 ☎ 041 720 581

🕐 Tue–Sun 9pm–midnight or later 🚤 Madonna dell'Orto

OPERA, BALLET AND THEATRE

Teatrino Groggia

Although it's a bit far out, in far-flung Sant'Alvise, this intimate little theatre is praised for its modern and contemporary productions and concerts. It provides a showcase for aspiring Italian writers, but also puts on the occasional production in English. Concerts range from traditional American folk to minimalist contemporary.

✉ Calle del Capitello, Cannaregio 3161 ☎ 041 524 4665 🚤 Sant'Alvise

Teatro Malibran

This was the city's original theatre, Teatro di San Giovanni Crisostomo, which has played a central role in cultural life since it was founded in 1678. It took its present name from Maria Malibran, who was a famous soprano of the early 19th century. After falling into disrepair by the 1970s, it underwent restoration and reopened in 2001, when it staged La Fenice productions. The theatre produces a programme of well-known operas, modern works, ballet and classical concerts.

✉ Calle dei Milion, Cannaregio 5873 ☎ 041 786 603, 041 786 601 (box office); www.teatrolafenice.it 🚤 Rialto

San Polo and Santa Croce

San Polo and Santa Croce make up much of central and western Venice, two large and ill-defined districts contained within the great curve of the Grand Canal.

San Polo, to the east, contains the better-known sights, notably the wonderful Rialto markets and Santa Maria Gloriosa dei Frari, Venice's largest church and most captivating religious building after

San Marco. Here, too, is the Scuola Grande di San Rocco, the most important of Venice's *scuole* (charitable foundations), which is also a shrine to the work of Tintoretto, one of the city's leading artists.

Santa Croce is altogether more peaceful, typified by venerable churches such as San Stae and San Giacomo dell'Orio and its sleepy square, and home to a handful of pleasant cafés and restaurants.

CA' PESARO

It's worth visiting if only to see inside this enormous 17th-century restored baroque *palazzo* overlooking the Grand Canal. It was built for Giovanni Pesaro, who became Doge in 1685, and now houses contemporary art exhibitions on the first two floors and Oriental art on the top floor. The Museo d'Arte Moderna was founded in 1902 with a handful of pedestrian pieces bought from the Biennale. The Museo d'Arte Orientale has a wealth of objects collected by Conti di Bardi during a trip to the Far East in the 19th century.
www.museicivicineneziani.it
🏠 6E ✉ Fondamenta Ca' Pesaro, Santa Croce 2076 ☎ Palace and museums 041 721 1127 🕒 Palace and museums Tue–Sun 10–5 ✋ Moderate, includes admission to palace and museums 🚤 San Stae

CAMPO SAN POLO

On the other side of the Grand Canal, the largest square is Campo San Polo, where the huge marble wellhead is a gathering place for the young on summer evenings.
🏠 17G 🚤 San Silvestro

MERCATO DI RIALTO

The oldest market in the Rialto is the fish market, located on the same site for over a thousand years. Today it is

housed in and around the lovely vaulted neo-Gothic Pescheria. Get here early before the crowds for the best atmosphere. Next to this is an array of fruit and vegetable stalls. The produce may have been shipped from the mainland, but its quality and taste are second to none. The prices are pretty good, too. The original traders and merchants lived in the warren of streets around here, which are bursting with butchers, bakers and purveyors of all kinds of foods.

🚌 8F ✉ Rialto 🕐 Mon–Sat 8–1; fish market is closed on Mon
🚤 Rialto

PALAZZO MOCENIGO

This was the home of one of the oldest and grandest Venetian families until recent years. The nine elegantly furnished rooms of the 17th-century *palazzo* provide a rare insight into 18th-century Venetian noble life. Richly gilded and painted, these rooms, with their fine furniture and Murano glass chandeliers, still have a private feeling about them. Many of the paintings, friezes and frescoes are by Jacopo Guarana. The building also houses a library and a collection of period costume (the Museo del Tessuto e Cotume), together with a small exhibition of antique Venetian textiles.

🚌 6E ✉ Salizzada San Stae, Santa Croce 1992 ☎ 041 721 798
🕐 Tue–Sun 10–4 💰 Moderate 🚤 San Stae

PONTE DI RIALTO

Built of Istrian stone in the late 16th century, this was, until 1854 when the Ponte dell'Accademia was completed, the only crossing of the Grand Canal that replaced an earlier wooden bridge. A single span, decorated with relief carvings and balustrades, it is famous for its parallel rows of shops facing one another on either side of the central path. These shops sell mostly jewellery, leather goods, silk and shoes. The bridge commands fine views of the canal, particularly in the direction of San Marco. At peak times the bridge can become very congested.

8F ✉ Canal Grande 🚤 Rialto

SAN CASSIANO

This sumptuous church, with its pillars draped in crimson and an attractive 13th-century campanile, is worth visiting for Tintoretto's majestic *Crucifixion* (1565–1568). The other two paintings by the artist have been heavily restored.

6E ✉ Campo San Cassiano, San Polo 1852 ☎ 041 721 408 ⊙ Apr–Sep daily 10–12, 5:30–7; Oct–Mar 10–12, 4:30–6 🎫 Free 🚤 San Stae/Rialto

SAN GIACOMO DELL'ORIO

This busy parish church is in a quiet *campo* in the west of the city, where the only visitors are likely to be those walking to the Piazzale Roma to catch a bus. Its architecture and decoration reflect the growth of Venice: pillars from Byzantium and one of the two 'ship's keel' roofs (like an inverted wooden ship) in Venice – the other is in Santo Stefano (➤ 89); paintings by Venetian masters; and, in comic contrast, a funny little relief carving of a knight – almost a cartoon character – on the outside wall.

➕ 5E ✉ Campo San Giacomo dell'Orio, Santa Croce ☎ 041 275 0462
🕐 Mon–Sat 10–5 ✋ Inexpensive 🚣 San Stae/Riva di Biasio

SAN GIACOMO DI RIALTO

Among the fruit and vegetable market stalls at the foot of the Rialto Bridge, this the oldest church in the city – said to have been founded in the early 5th century. It has grown many architectural and decorative curiosities, including a rare brick dome; over-large baroque altarpieces; and a large, 15th-century 24-hour clock on the façade. The church faces the market square, which was once used by bankers, money changers and insurance brokers.

➕ 8F ✉ Campo San Giacomo, San Polo 🕐 Mon–Sat 7–12, 3–6 ✋ Free
🚣 Rialto

SANTA MARIA GLORIOSA DEI FRARI

Best places to see, pages 50–51.

SAN NICOLÒ DA TOLENTINO

This colossal church with a vast, pillared Corinthian portico is close to the Piazzale Roma and is popular for weddings. Embedded in the exterior (under the porch) you can see a cannon ball, left by the Austrians during the siege of 1849. Inside, the church is elaborate, enriched with sculpture and paintings.

➕ 3F ✉ Campo dei Tolentini, Santa Croce 265 ☎ 041 522 2160
🕐 Daily 9–12, 4–6 ✋ Free 🚣 Piazzale Roma

SAN PANTALON

This typically Venetian baroque church probably makes a more immediate impact on the visitor than any church in Venice. On entering and looking up, the vast flat ceiling is painted with one enormous view of a mass ascent into Heaven. This startling scene also includes the life and martyrdom of San Pantalon and was painted at the end of the 17th century and the beginning of the 18th. A typically quirky Venetian postscript is the fate of the artist, Gian Antonio Fumiani, who, as he completed his work, stepped back to admire it better, fell from the scaffolding to his death and was buried in the church he had decorated so memorably. The church also contains smaller works by Veronese and Vivarini. Like several other Venetian churches, it has no façade as its builders ran out of money.

✚ 15H ✉ Campo San Pantalon, San Polo ☎ 041 523 5893 🕐 Mon–Sat 3–6 ✋ Free 🚤 San Tomà

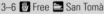

SAN POLO

The church stands in the largest square after San Marco. Its works of art include fine bronze statues of saints on the high altar and notable paintings by Tintoretto and both Tiepolos, including 14 paintings of The Stations of the Cross by the younger Tiepolo.

✚ 17G ✉ Campo San Polo, San Polo 2102 ☎ 041 275 0462 ✋ Mon–Sat 10–5 ✋ Inexpensive ⛴ San Silvestro/San Tomà

SAN STAE

Despite its handsome interior, this church is at its best viewed from the outside. Its neoclassical façade, decorated with joyous baroque statuary, provides one of the most striking views on the Grand Canal. Inside, the finest paintings are Tiepolo's *Martyrdom of St Bartholomew* and Piazzetta's *Martyrdom of St James the Great*. The church is used for art exhibitions and concerts.

✚ 6D ✉ Campo San Stae, Canal Grande, Santa Croce 1981 ☎ 041 275 0462 ✋ Mon–Sat 10–5 ✋ Inexpensive ⛴ San Stae

SCUOLA GRANDE DI SAN GIOVANNI EVANGELISTA

One of the six Scuole Grande and not generally open to the public but it is worth a visit for its splendid exterior. Located in a tiny square near the Frari, a beautiful Renaissance complex, it was designed by Mauro Codussi in 1454 and has a stunning archway designed by Pietro Lombardo in 1481. The eagle crowning the arch is the symbol of St John the Evangelist. The interior is remarkable for a converging double staircase that leads to the Albergo, the main conference room, hung with scenes from the life of St John. Admission to the building is possible when exhibitions or concerts are being held or sometimes on request.

✚ 4F ✉ Campiello de la Scuola, San Polo ☎ 041 718 8234 ✋ Occasionally open, check before visit ✋ Donation ⛴ San Tomà

SCUOLA GRANDE DI SAN ROCCO

Best places to see, pages 54–55.

HOTELS

Iris (€€)

In business since the 1930s, the Flora family hotel was refurbished in the late 1990s. Eighteen of the simply furnished 24 rooms have a private bathroom and all have air-conditioning. The highlight of this hotel is the pretty garden and the restaurant, Al Giardinetto, which serves excellent pizza and fish dishes, accompanied by live piano and jazz music.

✉ Fondemente dei Forner, San Polo 2910/A ☎ 041 522 2882; www.venice-hotel.irishotel.com 🚤 San Tomà

Locanda Sturion (€€–€€€)

Richly decorated in traditional Venetian style, the 11 rooms at this long-established hotel are supremely comfortable; two have Grand Canal views. The breakfast room overlooks the water and the hotel has its own restaurant.

✉ Calle del Sturion, San Polo 679 ☎ 041 523 6243; www.locandasturion.com 🚤 San Silvestro/Rialto

Marconi (€€–€€€)

You will have to get in quick to reserve one of the two rooms with a Grand Canal view but the other 24 do have an advantage – peace and quiet. This was considered an exclusive hotel in the 1930s and it has managed to retain some of that pre-war charm. Take a close-up view of the Rialto bridge over a coffee from one of the outdoor tables.

✉ Riva del Vin, San Polo 729 ☎ 041 522 2068; www.hotelmarconi.it 🚤 Rialto

San Cassiano-Ca' Favretto (€€–€€€)

In a converted 14th-century *palazzo* on the opposite side of the Grand Canal from the glorious Ca' d'Oro palace. Half the 35 rooms face the Grand Canal, the rest overlook at a side canal. This is a nice place to stay if you want something quieter and a retreat from the city's hustle and bustle.

✉ Calle della Rosa, Santa Croce 2232 ☎ 041 524 1768; www.sancassiano.it 🚤 San Stae

Tolentini (€–€€)

Tucked away en route from Piazzale Roma to the Frari, this an excellent budget choice. The rooms are a little small but the value and helpfulness of the staff make up for that. Very good reductions for on-line booking.

✉ Calle Amai, Santa Croce 197 ☎ 041 275 9140; www.albergotolentini.it
🚊 Piazzale Roma

RESTAURANTS

Ae Oche (€–€€)

A quirky and friendly pizzeria that actually has some good pizzas. With no wood-burning ovens allowed in the city it's not always easy to find a good example but this is one of the best.

✉ Calle delle Oche, Santa Croce 1552/A ☎ 041 524 1161 ⏱ Lunch, dinner
🚊 San Stae

Alla Madonna (€€€)

One of the oldest restaurants in the city and high on the list of Venetian favourites, especially for business meetings or family celebrations. Lots of space and plenty of typical local dishes including the seafood *ai frutte di mare*. Service can be a bit brusque; there's a quick turnover.

✉ Calle della Madonna, San Polo 594 ☎ 041 522 3824 (no reservations)
⏱ Lunch, dinner. Closed Wed 🚊 Rialto

Alla Zucca (€–€€)

Don't be fooled into thinking this is just another trattoria – there is an interesting twist in the cooking. Some dishes have an Asian theme, others a Mediterranean tang. Mainly vegetarian dishes and hence popular, so it's best to reserve ahead.

✉ Ponte del Megio, Calle del Tintor, Santa Croce 1762 ☎ 041 524 1570
⏱ Lunch, dinner. Closed Sun 🚊 San Stae

Al Ponte (€–€€)

Its nickname is La Patatina after the renowned large chips (fries) served here. Always very busy with locals and students, Al Ponte offers hearty food at a good price. Expect the popular seafood risotto and *polpette* (meatballs) to be on the menu.

✉ Ponte San Polo, San Polo 2741 ☎ 041 523 7238 🕔 Lunch, dinner. Closed
Sun 🚪 San Tomà

Antica Birraria la Corte (€€–€€€)

Set in a converted warehouse, this is something different for
Venice – contemporary and minimalist. Good quality food from
light bites to full meals.

✉ Campo San Polo, San Polo 2168 ☎ 041 275 0570 🕔 Lunch, dinner
🚪 San Silvestro

Antica Ostaria Ruga Rialto (€)

One of the best places for *cicheti*, which you can have at the bar
or in the room around the back. It's a popular joint with artists and
musicians and has occasional live music. Friendly staff.

✉ Ruga Rialto, San Polo 692 ☎ 041 521 1243 🕔 Lunch, dinner 🚪 Rialto

Antiche Carampane (€€€€)

A bit of a secret as it's hard to find, but seek it out and you
shouldn't be disappointed. Not one for the tourist menu; here you
will find traditional Venetian dishes (lots of fish) with a modern
twist. Be guided by the staff and enjoy the stories behind each
dish, as well as the food itself.

✉ Rio Terrà Carampane, San Polo 1911 ☎ 041 524 0165 🕔 Lunch, dinner.
Closed Sun, Mon 🚪 San Silvestro

Il Refolo (€€)

See page 59.

Vecio Fritolin (€)

See page 59.

SHOPPING

CERAMICS

Sabbie e Nebbie

This elegant little shop specialises in contemporary Italian
ceramics with clean, sleek and minimalist lines, influenced by

Japanese designs – they also stock pieces from Japan in muted tones and wonderful glazes.

✉ Calle dei Nomboli, San Polo 2768A ☎ 041 719 073 🚤 San Tomà

FASHION
Fate e Follette
There are adorably chic children's and baby clothes in this pretty shop opposite the Frari – kid's wear with a real Italian twist, the ideal shopping stop for doting grandparents.

✉ Campo dei Frari, San Polo 3006 ☎ 041 522 8336 🚤 San Tomà

Hibiscus
On the main drag from the Rialto to the Frari, this lovely women's-wear shop glows with the vibrant colours of easy-to-wear, well-cut jackets, shirts, tops and dresses in silks and fine cottons.

✉ Ruga Rialto, San Polo 1060–1061 ☎ 041 520 8899 🚤 San Silvestro

FOOD AND DRINK
Casa del Parmigiano
It may be small but this is said to be one of the best delis in Venice, and it's just a stone's throw from the Rialto markets. The selection of cheeses from all over Italy is as superb as it is mouthwatering. Homemade pastas, salamis, wines and olive oils – great for gifts.

✉ Erberia, San Polo 214–215 ☎ 041 520 6525 🚤 Rialto

Drogheria Mascari
A family business since 1948, this lovely shop is brimming with all manner of treats. There is a wondrous collection of wines, liqueurs, spices, teas, biscuits and special sweets and much, much more to tempt you with.

✉ Ruga Spezieri, San Polo 381 ☎ 041 522 9762 🚤 Rialto

LEATHER GOODS
Francis Model
A tiny leather shop where everything is made in the family workshop, as it has been for over 40 years. There are beautifully

crafted bags, briefcases in soft, supple leather as well as purses, wallets and belts.

✉ Ruga Rialto, San Polo 773A ☎ 041 521 2889 🚢 San Silvestro

WOODWORK
Gilberto Penzo

Gilberto Penzo is a world-renowned maker of replica wooden gondolas. This superb craftsman can turn his hand to other classic Venetian boats as well. If you can't afford the real thing, you can buy an inexpensive kit to make your own when you get home.

✉ Calle Seconda dei Saoneri, San Polo 2681 ☎ 041 719 372 🚢 San Tomà

ENTERTAINMENT

CINEMA
Arena di Campo Polo

From late July to early September the square is transformed into an open-air cinema.

✉ Campo San Polo, San Polo ☎ 041 524 1320 🚢 San Silvestro

CLASSICAL MUSIC
Basilica dei Frari

You will find a good mix of religious music, orchestral pieces and organ recitals.

✉ Campo dei Frari, San Polo ☎ 041 522 2637 🚢 San Tomà

Scuola Grande di San Rocco

With a musical tradition stretching back over 500 years, this is a superb setting to hear baroque music, featuring works by Monteverdi (1567–1643), long associated with the *scuola*.

✉ Campo San Rocco, San Polo 3052 ☎ 041 523 4864 🚢 San Tomà

NIGHTLIFE
Caffè dei Frari

Popular with students from the university, this is a great place for an aperitif before getting a meal nearby.

✉ Fondamenta dei Frari, San Polo 2564 ☎ 041 524 1877 🕓 Daily 9am–9pm
🚢 San Tomà

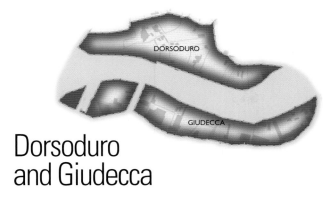

DORSODURO

GIUDECCA

Dorsoduro and Giudecca

Dorsoduro is the most easily identified of Venice's six *sestieri*, the arm of land that curves around the southern edge of the Grand Canal. A prosperous residential district, it contains the city's two principal art galleries – the modern art gallery, Collezione Peggy Guggenheim, and the Gallerie dell'Accademia, filled with the city's finest paintings, plus the Punta della Dogana, the old customs house, Venice's latest art space.

Also here is the great church of the Salute, one of the distinctive landmarks of the Grand Canal and the centrepiece of the view from San Marco and the Accademia bridge. Dorsoduro, as ever in Venice, is a lovely place to walk, with some particularly fine views from the Zattere, its southern waterfront. Among other things, you'll see La Giudecca, a long narrow island immediately across the water. Once a mostly working-class area, the island is now becoming increasingly chic.

ANGELO RAFFAELE

This church, one of the city's oldest foundations, is located in a secluded part of Dorsoduro. It is notable for its 18th-century organ decorated with paintings by Guardi.

✚ 13J ✉ Campo Angelo Raffaele ☎ 041 522 8548 ⏱ Daily 9–12, 3–5 ✋ Free ⛴ San Basilio

CA' REZZONICO

This immensely grand 17th-century palace overlooking the Grand Canal has been filled with furniture and paintings of the 18th century. The magnificent rooms of the piano nobile (main floor) are richly decorated with gilding, frescoes and painted ceilings, including one by Tiepolo. On the floor above you can see paintings of Venetian life by Guardi and Longhi as well as a succession of small rooms, decorated with frescoes by the younger Tiepolo. The top floor, which houses a collection of costumes, the stock of a pharmacist's shop and a marionette theatre, is often closed.

The poet Robert Browning occupied a suite of rooms below the piano nobile (not open to the public) from 1888 until his death here in 1889.

www.museiciviciveneziani.it

✚ 15J ✉ Fondamenta Rezzonico, Dorsoduro 3136 ☎ 041 241 0100 ⏱ Apr–Oct Wed–Mon 10–6; Nov–Mar 10–5 (ticket office closes 1 hour earlier) ✋ Expensive ⛴ Ca' Rezzonico

CAMPO SAN BARNABA

Perhaps the most charmingly Venetian of all the squares is the Campo San Barnaba near the Accademia Gallery. Presided over by the noble façade of the church of San Barnaba (a simple parish church with an air of tranquillity) this *campo* bustles with life: shops, two cafés with tables outside and a barge selling the world's most photographed fruit and vegetables moored in the canal that connects with the Grand Canal.

➕ 15J 🚤 Ca' Rezzonico

CAMPO SANTA MARGHERITA

More lively is the Campo Santa Margherita, where vendors sell fruit, vegetables, fish and shoes, and local Venetian life goes on undisturbed by crowds of tourists.

➕ 14H 🚤 Ca' Rezzonico

COLLEZIONE PEGGY GUGGENHEIM

The collection of Cubist, Abstract and Surrealist art acquired by the late Peggy Guggenheim, the American millionairess, is housed in her former home, an unfinished 18th-century *palazzo* on the Grand Canal, Palazzo Venier de Leoni. This is the perfect antidote to a superfluity of Byzantine, Gothic Renaissance and baroque art. Paintings and sculptures of the 20th century – including Peggy Guggenheim's own discovery, the energetic Jackson Pollock – will delight those who appreciate modern art, while those who do not will enjoy the view from the garden, overlooking the Grand Canal. Be sure to view Marino Marini's *Angel of the Citadel* on the terrace. This is one of the world's most important 20th-century collections outside the US.

www.guggenheim-venice.it

✚ 17K ✉ Calle San Cristoforo, Dorsoduro 701 ☎ 041 240 5411
🕐 Apr–Oct Wed–Mon 10–6; Nov–Mar 10–6 💷 Expensive
🚤 Accademia/Salute

DOGANA DI MARE

This stands where the Dorsoduro district of Venice (to the east of the church of the Salute ➤ 52–53) juts out like a ship's prow into the lagoon at the junction of the Grand Canal and the Basin of San Marco. On top of its tower stand two bronze figures of Atlas holding up a golden globe surmounted by a figure of Fortune as a wind vane. Behind the tower are the 17th-century Customs warehouses. You can stop for a moment and enjoy the views of San Marco and over the lagoon.

✚ 19K ✉ Dorsoduro 🕐 See page 150 🚤 Salute

GALLERIE DELL'ACCADEMIA

Best places to see, pages 40–41.

PEGGY
GUGGENHEIM
COLLECTION

GESUATI

Also known as Santa Maria del Rosario, the Gesuati takes its popular name from a religious order of the same name founded at the end of the 14th century, but suppressed in 1688. The order built a small oratory on the site, later adapted and enlarged by the Dominicans into the present church (consecrated in 1736). Its artistic highlights are three ceiling frescoes by Giambattista Tiepolo, depicting scenes from the story of the Dominican order (1737–39).

www.chorusvenezia.org

✚ 16L ✉ Fondamenta delle Zattere ai Gesuati, Dorsoduro 917 ☎ 041 275 0462, 041 523 0625 🕐 Mon–Sat 10–5 💰 Inexpensive 🚢 Zattere

GIUDECCA

The island of the Giudecca lies to the south of central Venice across the wide, deep-water Canale della Giudecca. Originally a chain of small islands, it was settled by a small Jewish community, which lived here until the establishment of the Ghetto (➤ 119). It has always been a popular place to escape the summer heat, even as early as the 13th century when wealthy aristocrats built splendid palaces surrounded by gardens. Subsequently, in the 19th and 20th centuries it became an industralized area with the creation of factories and shipyards. This has declined over the last 50 years and today it is primarily a residential area. The main sights are on the north side of the island, including the Redentore (➤ 151), the Zittelle and Sant'Eufemia churches. Here you will also find bars and restaurants, food shops and examples of 14th-century *palazzi*.

✠ 14M 🚤 Palanca/Redentore/Zitelle

a walk around Dorsoduro

Start on the south side of the bridge, facing the Gallerie dell'Accademia (➤ 40–41). Turn left into Rio Terrà Antonio Foscarini and continue to the waterfront, passing the church of the Gesuati with its ceiling and altar paintings by Tiepolo.

Turn right at the end along the Zattere, turning right just before the bridge. Continue along by the canal. On your left is the boatyard of Squero di San Trovaso (➤ 154) and the church of the same name (➤ 153). Take a left at the second bridge into Calle Toletta and continue straight on crossing another bridge into Campo San Barnaba

(➤ 143). Take the left corner out of the square, cross the first bridge into Rio Terrà Canal and turn left into Sant' Aponal. Turn right into Campo Santa Margherita.

This square is a pleasant place to stop for lunch or a rest.

Return to Sant' Aponal and continue along, turning right by the Scuola Grande (➤ 153) and the church of Santa Maria dei Carmini (➤ 151). Turn left by the canal and follow the

Fondamenta Soccorso to the junction with the next canal. Turn left and cross the second bridge to the church of San Sebastiano (▶ 152). Skirt the right hand side of the church and cross the broad campo to the back of the church of Angelo Raffaele (▶ 142).

Look out for the statue of Angel, Tobias and his dog over the main entrance of the church. The large open *campo* is a good place for a rest.

Cross the bridge in front of the church and turn right. Follow this fondamenta past four bridges until the canal turns sharply left. Turn the corner and continue to the next bridge on the right. Cross this and follow Calle Sbiacca. Turn right, then left and cross another bridge. Turn right. Take the first left after the next bridge; you will see the back of the Scuola Grande di San Rocco (▶ 153) ahead of you. Cross the bridge, bear right along the side of the scuola and the glorious church of the Frari lies ahead.

Distance 3.5km (2 miles)
Time 2 hours plus stops
Start point Ponte dell'Accademia ✚ 16K
End point Santa Maria Gloriosa dei Frari ✚ 15G
Lunch Campo Santa Margherita (▶ 143) is a lively square with a choice of restaurants and cafés

PONTE DELL'ACCADEMIA

This is the widest crossing of the Grand Canal and surely the bridge with the loveliest of views. The canal's gentle curves, the boats and gondolas sail beneath you and the view of the dome of the Salute (➤ 52–53) is magical.

✚ 16K ✉ Canal Grande 🚢 Accademia

PUNTA DELLA DOGANA

In 2009, the 17th-century customs warehouses of the Dogana del Mare (➤ 144) opened as Venice's most important contemporary art exhibition space. On behalf of the Fondazione François Pinhault, who also run the Grassi (➤ 83), the interior space was transformed by the Japanese architect Tadao Ando, into a huge, high space, sleekly blending with the original building. Part of the Pinhault contemporary art collection is permanently on view and it's also used for temporary exhibitions.

✚ 19K ✉ Campo della Salute, Dorsoduro ☎ 199 139 139 🕐 Wed–Mon 10–7 ✋ Expensive 🚢 Salute

IL REDENTORE

This is best seen across the water from the centre of Venice. Indeed, its architect, Palladio, who was commissioned to design it as an act of thanksgiving for the ending of a 16th-century plague, intended it to catch and hold the distant eye. The façade and the interior together form a magnificent example of what came to be known as Palladian architecture. On the third Sunday of July, a bridge of boats is constructed across the Giudecca Canal for the celebration of the Feast of the Redeemer (Redentore). The church is dramatically floodlit at night.

✚ 20M (off map) ✉ Campo del Redentore, Giudecca Island 195 ☎ 041 523 1415 🕔 Mon–Sat 10–5, Sun 1–5; closed Sun in Jul and Aug ✋ Inexpensive
🚤 Redentore

SANTA MARIA DEI CARMINI

Near the Campo Santa Margherita, this is a large and sombre 14th-century church, displaying many fine paintings, including a series in the nave illustrating the history of the Carmelite Order.

✚ 14J ✉ Campo dei Carmini, Dorsoduro ☎ 041 522 6553 🕔 Mon–Sat 2:30–5:30 ✋ Free 🚤 San Basilio/ Ca' Rezzonico

SANTA MARIA DELLA SALUTE
Best places to see, pages 52–53.

SAN NICOLÒ DEI MENDICOLI
This ornate yet modest parish church in a poor district of the city near the docks is one of Venice's oldest. Restored by British contributions to the Venice in Peril Fund in 1977, its gilded wooden statues gleam anew. Built between the 12th and 15th centuries and well-stocked with statuary and paintings, it is a good goal when exploring the hinterland of the western end of the Zattere and visiting the nearby churches of San Sebastiano and Angelo Raffaele.

🔶 13J (off map) ✉ Campo San Nicolò, Dorsoduro 1907 ☎ 041 275 0382
🕐 Mon–Sat 10–12, 4–6 ✋ Inexpensive
🚤 San Basilio/Ca' Rezzonico

SAN SEBASTIANO
The most important of the three major churches near the docks, it belongs to the great painter Paolo Veronese, who decorated it and is buried there. His works are everywhere in the church, including the open doors of the organ and the ceiling, in the chancel, the sacristy and the gallery, where he painted frescoes on the walls. In all, he painted here the richest and most comprehensive exhibition of his own

PAVLO CALIARIO
NATVRÆ ÆMVLO
SV ERST TE FAT S

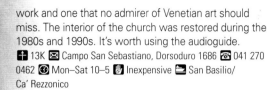

work and one that no admirer of Venetian art should miss. The interior of the church was restored during the 1980s and 1990s. It's worth using the audioguide.

✠ 13K ✉ Campo San Sebastiano, Dorsoduro 1686 ☎ 041 270 0462 🕐 Mon–Sat 10–5 ✋ Inexpensive 🚤 San Basilio/ Ca' Rezzonico

SAN TROVASO

This is a huge Palladian church with two identical façades because, it is said, two rival 16th-century families each wanted to be the first to enter and so could do so simultaneously. The interior is lofty, light and peaceful; outside, the *campo* is a pleasant place to sit in the sun away from the city bustle.

✠ 15K ✉ Campo San Trovaso, Dorsoduro 1098 ☎ 041 522 2133 🕐 Mon–Fri 8–11, 3–6, Sat 8–11, 3–7, Sun 8.30–1 ✋ Free 🚤 Accademia/Zattere

SCUOLA GRANDE DEI CARMINI

This is the Venetian headquarters of the Carmelite order, founded in Palestine in 1235. Here the nuns undertake charitable work and attend services at the nearby church (► 151). The Carmini had Giambattista Tiepolo (the elder) as its principal decorator in the 18th century and his flamboyant ceilings are the highlight of this *scuola*. His panels are in the Salone, on the upper floor, accessed via a stuccoed staircase. Although the themes are religious, his painting is sensual. They are not easy to understand but are based around the Carmelite emblem, the scapular, and are audacious works of art and a triumph of trompe l'oeil perspective.

✠ 14J ✉ Campo dei Carmini, Dorsoduro 2617 ☎ 041 528 9420 🕐 Mar–Oct Thu–Tue 10–5, Nov–Feb 11–4 ✋ Moderate 🚤 Ca' Rezzonico

SQUERO DI SAN TROVASO

This is a picturesque boatyard where gondolas have been built and repaired for hundreds of years, and it is still full of activity. Even though it is closed to the public you can get great photographs of the upturned gondolas awaiting repair, with the church of San Trovaso as a backdrop, all from the opposite side of the canal.

✚ 15K ✉ On San Trovaso Canal (near the Zattere), Dorsoduro 🚤 Zattere

ZATTERE

The Zattere forms a series of *fondamente* (quayside) along the Canal della Giudecca on the southern side of Dorsoduro. It stretches from the Stazione Márittima in the west to the Punta della Dogana in the east, its name deriving from the unloading of heavy goods – particulary cargos of salt for the nearby warehouses – which were floated to the quayside on rafts known as *záttere*. Ventians now love to take the *passeggiata* here and it is a great place to rest, have a drink or an ice cream.

✚ 15L ✉ Zattere, Dorsoduro 🚤 Zattere/San Basilio

HOTELS

Accademia-Villa Maravege (€€€)

This is a 17th-century house in its own garden at the junction of two canals, just off the Grand Canal, which once housed the Russian Embassy. Its position is idyllic, particularly when the wisteria is in bloom, and it is convenient for districts away from the tourist trails. Rooms are nicely furnished but can be small.

✉ Fondamenta Bollani, Dorsoduro 1058 ☎ 041 521 0188; www.pensioneaccademia.it 🚤 Accademia

American (€€–€€€)

Recently refurbished, the rooms are now light and airy. The hotel is located by a pretty and quiet canal and has the added bonus of a garden. A good choice away from the crowds. The staff is helpful and even arrange a babysitting service and reservations for tours.

✉ Fondamenta Bragadin, Dorsoduro 628 ☎ 041 520 4733; www.hotelamerican.com 🚤 Accademia

Calcina (€€)

See page 74.

Ca' Maria Adele (€€€€€)

Ideally placed near the beautiful church of Santa Maria della Salute and the *vaparetto* stop, this is luxury personified. With only seven rooms and seven suites you choose your themed room from cosy to Oriental.

✉ Rio Terrà dei Catecumeni, Dorsoduro 111 ☎ 041 520 3078; www.camariadele.it 🚤 Salute

Cipriani (€€€€)

See page 74.

La Galleria (€€)

See page 75.

Locanda Ca' Foscari (€)

This is a good bet if you are on a limited budget. Not all the 10

rooms have their own bathroom but everything is clean and bright.
And it does a good breakfast.

✉ Calle della Frescada, Dorsoduro 3887/B ☎ 041 710 401;
www.locandacafoscari. com 🚤 San Tomà

RESTAURANTS

Al Bottegon (€)
See page 58.

Altanella (€€€)
A pleasant place to go on a trip to the island of Giudecca with its
waterside terrace, and quiet setting. Good fresh fish. Service can
be slow but it's worth the wait.

✉ Calle delle Erbe, Giudecca 268 ☎ 041 522 7780 🕐 Lunch, dinner. Closed
Mon, Tue and 2 weeks in Aug 🚤 Palanca

Casin di Nobili (€€–€€€)
Best known for its pizzas, Casin di Nobili has a good range of
alternatives on the menu. You can sit out in the pretty garden
in summer.

✉ Campo San Barnaba, Dorsoduro 2765 ☎ 041 241 1841 🕐 Lunch, dinner.
Closed Mon 🚤 Ca' Rezzonico

Harry's Dolci (€€€)
Over on Giudecca island, the same management has a restaurant
that serves much the same sort of food as Harry's Bar, but with
the emphasis on desserts and cakes. There are wonderful views
from the outside tables, situated right beside the water .

✉ Fondamenta San Biagio, Giudecca 773 ☎ 041 522 4844 🕐 Lunch, dinner.
Closed Mon dinner, Tue and Nov–end Apr 🚤 Palanca

Locanda Montin (€€€)
Among the best-known garden restaurants. It is difficult to find, in
a quiet and charming district near the Campo San Barnaba, but so
popular that reservations are essential.

✉ Fondamento di Borgo, Dorsoduro 1147 ☎ 041 522 7151 🕐 Lunch, dinner.
Closed Tue, Wed 🚤 Ca' Rezzonico/Accademia

Mistrà (€–€€)
See page 59.

Nico (€)
See page 59.

SHOPPING

BOOKS

Libreria Toletta e Toletta Studio

The Libreria carries a huge range of beautiful illustrated books on Venice, as well as art and cookery books, often at 20–40 per cent discounts. Across the *calle*, the Studio has posters, art books and interesting small gifts.

✉ Calle Toletta, Dorsoduro 1214 ☎ 041 523 2034 🚏 Ca' Rezzonico

JEWELLERY

Antiquariato Oggetistica Claudia Canestrelli

Tucked away near the Guggenheim, this tiny shop is a treasure house of small antiques and custom-made jewellery. The owner bases her designs on 18th-century patterns, producing pretty and eminently wearable earrings and necklaces. Get 10 per cent discount for cash.

✉ Campiello Barbaro, Dorsoduro 364A ☎ 041 522 7072 🚏 Salute

Studio Genninger

Beautiful costume jewellery made using glass beads is on offer here – the designs are far from traditional and the imagination of this American designer shines through in her work.

✉ Calle del Traghetto, Dorsoduro 2793/A ☎ 041 522 5565; www.genningerstudio.com 🚏 Ca' Rezzonico

LINENS AND TABLEWARE

Annelie

There's a wonderful range of surprisingly inexpensive good quality lace products at this little shop near San Barnaba. You'll find pretty ready-to-wear clothes for children and adults, nightwear, tablecloths with embroidery and lace insets, towels, napkins and storage bags in cotton, silk and linen – ideal souvenirs of Venice.

✉ Calle Lunga San Barnaba, Dorsoduro 2748 ☎ 041 520 3277

🖻 Ca' Rezzonico

SHOES
Risuola di Giovanni Dittura

This old-fashioned shoe store near the Accademia has one of the best (and cheapest!) ranges of *friulani*, the traditional Venetian velvet slippers, in the city. Jewel-bright colours and comfort make them wonderful for casual evening wear.

✉ Calle Nuova Sant'Agnesi, Dorsoduro 871 ☎ 041 5231163 🖻 Accademia

ENTERTAINMENT

CLASSICAL MUSIC
Santa Maria della Salute

A wonderful venue for organ music. Listen during Sunday Mass at 11am to the resident organist or to visiting guest performers.

✉ Campo della Salute, Dorsoduro ☎ 041 522 5558 🖻 Salute

NIGHTLIFE
Il Caffè

Another popular haunt that stays open later than most and is located in a lovely square. Popular for coffee by day, it becomes the focal point of the *campo* at night.

✉ Campo Santa Margherita, Dorsoduro 2963 ☎ 041 528 7998 🕐 Mon–Sat 7.30am–2am 🖻 Ca' Rezzonico

Margaret Duchamp

This is one of the liveliest bars in the city, and you can get a good choice of beer here plus a reasonable selection of wines.

✉ Campo Santa Margherita, Dorsoduro 3019 ☎ 041 528 6255 🕐 Sun–Fri 9am–2am, Sat 5pm–2am 🖻 Ca' Rezzonico

Piccolo Mondo

Known as El Suk, this intimate, upmarket club has been pulling in a well-heeled crowd to dance until late since the 1970s.

✉ Calle Contarini Corfu, Dorsoduro 1056 ☎ 041 520 0371 🖻 San Tomà

Lagoon Islands

Scattered across nearly 500sq km (200sq miles) of the Venetian lagoon are around 40 islands. Some have a proud history of their own; some were famous for their industries; others were renowned as religious centres.

Many of them acted as fortresses, gunpowder factories and stores; others were hospitals and asylums. Half of them are now deserted, while those still inhabited may be thriving communities or isolated institutions – a prison, a hospital or a religious retreat – and a few are used for public or private recreation. Some provide the fertile ground for vegetable crops to supply the Rialto's markets. Enough of them can be visited to add another dimension to a holiday in Venice. The main islands are well-serviced by *vaporetto*, but others can only be reached by the more expensive water taxis.

BURANO

The fishermen's and lace makers' island with a
population of about 5,000 lies more than 8km (5 miles)
to the northeast of Venice. While Murano (▶ 162–163)
is workaday and slightly dishevelled, Burano is neat and
clean and its multi-coloured cottages lining little canals
make it a perfect subject for photographs. Its character
has been shaped by its industries – the robust way of life
of its fishermen and boatbuilders and the delicacy of its
lace makers' skills. Usually women can be seen making
lace outside the doors of their cottages – although they
are now dwindling in number – and their products (as
well as embroidery from Hong Kong) are on sale at stalls

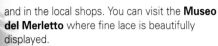

and in the local shops. You can visit the **Museo del Merletto** where fine lace is beautifully displayed.

There are few buildings of note, but the church of **San Martino** contains a huge and disturbing painting of the *Crucifixion* by the elder Tiepolo and has the most alarmingly tilted campanile of them all.

🚤 LN from Fondamente Nuove

Museo del Merletto

✉ Piazza Galuppi 187 ☎ 041 730 034 🕐 Apr–Oct Wed–Mon 10–5; Nov–Mar 10–4 ✋ Moderate

San Martino

✉ Piazza Galuppi ☎ 041 730 096 🕐 Daily 8–12, 3–7 ✋ Free

CHIOGGIA

Once an island, Chioggia is now, like Venice, connected to the mainland by a causeway; unlike Venice, several of its canals have been filled in to become roads for cars. In the far south of the lagoon, 26km (16 miles) from Venice, it has grown from a fishing port to an important town of some 55,000 inhabitants. Now, in essence, it belongs to the mainland rather than the lagoon.

Much of the town, particularly around the remaining canals, is reminiscent of Venice, and many buildings date from the 13th to 18th centuries. There are several fine churches, notably the Duomo, built between the 13th and 17th centuries, which contains a painting by the elder Tiepolo. There are a number of excellent fish restaurants near the harbour and in the Corso del Popolo.

🚌 From Piazzale Roma 🚤 11 from the Lido

ℹ Museo Civico, Fondamenta San Francesco ☎ 041 550 0911

LIDO DI VENEZIA

This is the only one of the Venetian islands to have roads, and its buses, cars and lorries are imported by ferry from the mainland. A little to the southeast of Venice, it is just over 11km (7 miles) long and 1km (half a mile) wide, covering the largest sand bank between the lagoon and the Adriatic. With a population of about 20,000, it is essentially a seaside holiday resort and is crowded in summer, when it is also host to the International Film Festival.

It was at its most fashionable before World War I as the architecture of its hotels and villas testifies, and its long sandy beach is still lined with the old wooden bathing-huts. Look for some interesting art nouveau and art deco buildings. Of particular interest on the Gran Viale is the Hungaria Palace and No 14, the Villa Monplaisir. Another striking building is the Grand Hotel Excelsior Palace (➤ 170), sporting its very own minaret. There's also the historic church of San Nicolò, founded in 1044, at the northern end of the island. The doge came here on Ascension Day after the ceremony of marrying Venice to the sea.

From the *vaporetto* bound from the Lido to San Marco, Venice is seen as it was intended it should first be seen, from the deck of a ship approaching from the sea, its towers, domes and palaces materializing between water and sky in one of the great spectacles of the world.

🚌 ACTV buses leave for all destinations on the Lido 🚤 1 from San Zaccaria or stops on the Grand Canal

🛈 Viale Santa Maria Elisabetta 6/a, Lido di Venezia ☎ 041 526 5721

🕓 Jun–Sep daily 8:30–7:30

MURANO

With around 5,000 inhabitants, Murano lies a short distance to the north of the city. It is an industrial island and has the feel of a small working town, although some of its factories lie derelict. Glass is its product and has been since the 13th century, when production was moved out of Venice itself because of the fire risk. Venetian glass has long been a curious mixture of the beautiful and the vulgar, whether in table-glass, ornaments, mirrors or chandeliers. Past products can be viewed in the **Museo del Vetro,** together with a history of glass on the island. New production can be seen in many factory showrooms.

Murano is a miniature, shabbier Venice with its own scaled-down Canal Grande, crossed by a single bridge. Its most notable building is the church of **Santa Maria e Donato,** which has a 12th-century mosaic floor and a 15th-century 'ship's keel' roof.
41 or DM

Museo del Vetro
Fondamenta Giustinian 8 ☎ 041 739 586 Apr–Oct Thu–Tue 10–6; Nov–Mar 10–5 Moderate To Museo

Santa Maria e Donato
Campo San Donato ☎ 041 739 056 Mon–Sat 9–12, 3:30–7, Sun 3:30–7 Free To Museo

SAN FRANCESCO DEL DESERTO

This remote and peaceful island can be reached by water taxi from
Burano, and the resident friars will show visitors the 13th-century
cloister and the church of the hermitage, where St Francis of
Assisi is said to have stayed.

www.isola-sanfrancescodeldeserto.it

☎ 041 528 6863 ⏱ Irregular hours; phone or see website for details
✋ Donation on admission 🚤 Water taxi from ✉ Burano

SAN LAZZARO DEGLI ARMENI

This Armenian island can be visited to see the church, library and
monastery where Lord Byron stayed in 1817 to learn Armenian.

☎ 041 526 0104 ⏱ Daily guided tour 3:25–4:25 ✋ Moderate 🚤 20

SAN MICHELE

This is the cemetery island, as can be seen by its sepulchral white walls and the tall, dark cypress trees beyond. The beautiful 15th-century church of San Michele in Isola is of interest to students of Renaissance artchitecture, but the cemetery is even sadder than could be expected, for dead Venetians cannot rest there long. While the famous – such as the composer Stravinsky, the poet Ezra Pound and the ballet impresario Diaghilev – are allowed to remain, nearly all Venetians buried here are disinterred after a period and their bones scattered on a reef made of their ancestors' remains in a remote reach of the lagoon. Visitors cannot fail to appreciate that here death, as well as life, is transitory.

🚤 41, 42 to Cimitero (cemetery)

TORCELLO

If you only visit one island make it Torcello. It was the first island to be settled by refugees from the barbarian invasion of the 5th century. At the height of its power, the population was said to have numbered 20,000, but the growth of the more distant and secure Venice, the silting of its creek and the prevalence of malaria reduced it to the level of the other small islands of the lagoon by the 15th century. Now the permanent popluation is only around 20 people, increased slighty in the summer by restaurant staff.

Lying close to the mainland marshes and more than 10 km (6 miles) to the northeast of Venice, the little green island offers peace after the bustling city and relaxation in walks along its narrow footpaths. Its great monument is the cathedral of **Santa Maria dell'Assunta,** where the extraordinary Byzantine mosaics – notably a tall and compelling Madonna and Child and a vast depiction of Judgement Day – have been restored. The basilica dates from 638 and is the oldest building in Venice. It remains virtually untouched since alterations in the 11th century.

The whole island, including the cathedral, the small church of Santa Fosco, the archaeological museum, **Museo dell'Estuario** and the surrounding farmland, is easily explored and can be combined with lunch on a day-trip from Venice without making an early start or expecting a late return.

🚤 LN from Fondamente Nuove, 'T' from Burano

Basilica di Santa Maria dell'Assunta

✉ Torcello ☎ 041 296 0630, 041 521 2362 🕐 Mar–Oct daily 10:30–6; Nov–Feb 10–5 💶 Moderate

Museo dell'Estuario

✉ Torcello ☎ 041 730 761 🕐 Mar–Oct Tue–Sun 10:30–5.30; Nov–Feb 10–5 💶 Moderate

a boat trip around the Isole Venezia

In the Lagoon north of Venice is an archipelago of flat little islands. Many of these are uninhabited or privately owned, but some have been populated for centuries. Three – Murano, Burano and Torcello – each in a very different way, are interesting places to visit on a day trip from Venice.

From San Zaccaria the boat heads southeast past the island of San Giorgio Maggiore.

The church here (1559–80), by Palladio, contains works by Tintoretto and has excellent views from its bell tower.

The boat then chugs round the eastern peninsula of Venice before heading northwest, past the Isola di San Michele.

The island has been used as a graveyard since the 19th century; Ezra Pound Diaghilev and Stravinsky are among those who lie behind its protective walls.

North of here is the island of Murano.

The centre of Venetian glass-blowing since the 13th century, Murano has numerous factories offering guided tours and the Museo del Vetro with glass pieces from the 15th century onward. This island is like a miniature Venice with its own Grand Canal.

Next comes Burano.

Once a great lace-making hub, Burano is now more remarkable for its brightly painted houses – purple, sky blue, leaf green and more – and the alarmingly leaning tower of San Martino church. Walk in the back streets to avoid the crowds and you will see that time has stood still, the washing still hangs out and the locals tend their pretty balconies and pots of bright flowers.

Torcello, the last, is the most historic, reached by the 'T' shuttle boat from Burano.

Torcello was once a thriving community of 20,000, but started to decline in the 14th century. Now all that remain are two adjoining churches set in serene rural scenery near an old canal. The 9th- to 11th-century Cathedral of Santa Maria dell'Assunta has a charmingly expressive mosaic of the Last Judgement, while the 12th-century church of Santa Fosca is surrounded on three sides by a harmonious peristyle (row of columns) and has a tranquil, simple interior.

Distance 20km (12 miles)
Time Allow about 2.5–3 hours without stops; up to a day with stops
Start/end point San Zaccaria *vaparetto* stop ✚ 21J
Lunch Locanda Cipriani (➤ 59)

HOTELS

Quattro Fontane (€€–€€€)

This is among the nicest of the smaller hotels on the Lido, with 60 rooms in a chalet-style building, a stone's throw from the water. The public areas are attractively furnished with antiques, and meals are served in the garden, where you'll also find a tennis court.

✉ Via Quattro Fontane 16, Lido di Venezia ☎ 041 526 0227; www.quattrofontane.com ③ Apr–mid-Nov 🚤 Lido Santa Maria Elisabetta

Soffiador (€)

You can stay on Murano at this friendly, relaxed, family-run hotel. Rooms are simple and a good size, there's the bonus of enjoying Murano once the day tourists have gone away, while the prices make it a superb choice if you're watching the budget.

✉ Viale Brassagio 10, Murano ☎ 041 739 430; www.venicehotel.it 🚤 Faro

RESTAURANTS

Al Gatto Nero (€€–€€€)

Off the main tourist trail, this traditional and friendly trattoria offers simply but expertly cooked fresh fish plus a selection of Buranese dishes, including *risotto all buranella* (rice with seafood).

✉ Fondamenta della Guidecca 88, Burano ☎ 041 730 120 ③ Lunch, dinner. Closed Mon 🚤 Burano LN

Alla Maddelena (€€)

See page 58.

Busa alla Torre (€€)

See page 59.

Locanda Cipriani (€€€)

See page 59.

SHOPPING

GLASS

Davide Penso

Come here to find what Venetian glass jewellery makers are doing in the 21st century – immensely wearable necklaces, earrings and bracelets with a modern twist come in myriad colours and finishes, so subtle it's hard to believe they're glass. Davide Penso is considered one of the world's best beadmakers.

✉ Fondamenta Cavour 48, Murano ☎ 041 527 4634; www.davidepenso.com
🚢 Murano Venier

Mazzega

The best in elegant table glassware can be bought in this shop in Murano. They also give demonstrations of glass sculpture and chandelier production.

✉ Fondamenta da Mula 147, Murano ☎ 041 736 888; www.mazzega.it
🚢 Murano DM (Museo/Venier)

Rossana e Rossana

Traditional Venetian glass-making combined with contemporary design. High quality produced with superb technique and crafts-manship. Choose from vases, glasses, frames and wonderful replicas of shells, oysters and sea creatures.

✉ Riva Lunga 11, Murano ☎ 041 527 4076; www.ro-e-ro.com 🚢 Murano DM (Venier)

LACE
Emilia

Lace is still made on Burano, and this shop has some exquisite examples, used to trim underwear, bed linen and handkerchiefs. Prices are extremely high, but they also sell good imported lace and organise lace-making demonstrations.

✉ Piazza Baldassare Galuppi 205, Burano ☎ 041 735 299 🚢 Burano LN

ENTERTAINMENT

CINEMA
Palazzo del Cinema

Home to Venice's Film Festival (► 25). Tickets go quickly for the premières. Also hosts fashion shows.

✉ Lungomare Marconi 90, Lido ☎ 041 521 8711; www.labiennale.org
🚢 Lido 1

Excursions

ASOLO

The most beautiful of the hinterland towns, Asolo lies in the foothills of the Alps 64km (40 miles) from Venice. A charming town of some 6,000 inhabitants, its old houses – sometimes arcaded at street level as is the custom in hill towns – cluster around squares and narrow streets and overlook a landscape of villas and cypress trees.

www.turismo.provinciatreviso.it

🚌 No direct bus to Asolo. Train to Bassano del Grappa, then bus towards Montebelluna and a shuttle to Asolo. Car or tour easiest

ℹ️ Piazza Garibaldi 73 ☎ 0423 529 046

BASSANO DEL GRAPPA

In the foothills of the Alps, nearly 80km (50 miles) north-west of Venice, this town of 37,000 inhabitants was once under Venetian rule. Formerly renowned for its school of painting, it now produces colourful pottery, which is sold in Venice and throughout northern Italy.

There are some fine old buildings and a famous covered wooden bridge – the Ponte degli Coperto – that has been rebuilt several times since the early 13th century. Bassano is noted for the strong alcoholic spirit, grappa. The town is a good base for exploring the mountains – particularly Monte Grappa, which was an Italian stronghold during World War I – and the battlefields Ernest Hemingway described in *A Farewell to Arms*.

Farther north and into the Alps is the handsome old town of Belluno and beyond it the Dolomite mountains and the celebrated resort of Cortina, renowned for winter sports and summer walking. Austria is also just within range of a day's excursion.

www.provincia.vicenza.it

🚉 From Venezia San Lucia station

ℹ️ Largo Corona d'Italia 35 ☎ 0424 524 351

BELLUNO

This attractive town, the capital of Belluno province and 90km (56 miles) from Venice, is at the junction of the flat plains of Veneto to the south and the stunning Dolomite mountains to the north. It claimed the accolade of 'Alpine Town of the Year in 1999' but it is often overlooked by people in their rush to see the mountains. There is much more to Belluno than being the starting point for a hiking weekend in summer or a skiing holiday in winter. Its architecture reflects its close proximity to Venice and merges well with the rural style of the surrounding countryside. Highlights of the town include the spectacular views from the 12th-century Porta Rugo and from the bell tower of the 16th-century Duomo. Take a break in the town's finest square, Piazza del Mercato, complete with fountain and arcaded Renaissance palaces.

www.infodolomiti.it

🚆 From Venezia San Lucia station

ℹ️ Piazza Duomo 2 ☎ 0437 940 083

DOLOMITI

The Dolomite mountains look as if they've been carved, folded and squeezed into an extraordinary variety of gnarled crags. They are named after Frenchman Déodat Tancrè Gratet de Domomieu (1750–1801), who was responsible for discovering the chemical component that renders the local rock so different from others. Although this is Italy, the language, scenery, architecture and much of the culture have been strongly influenced by Austria, and in particular in the north of the region, on the far side of the Dolomites, nearly all the place names have versions in German.

It is possible to take tours from Venice to the mountains, where you will witness soaring peaks, deep verdant valleys, emerald lakes and enchanting mountain villages. Some tours take you as far as Cortina d'Ampezzo, one of Italy's top ski and alpine resorts. There are plenty of superb photo opportunities. Activities in the mountains include rambling along the footpaths and picnicking, mountain biking, skiing in season and the use of chairlifts to get to see some of the most breathtaking scenery. The range of flora is extensive: look for the gorgeous orange mountain lily, pretty saxigfrages, the purple gentian (among a dozen gentian species) – the roots of which are used to make a local liqueur – the black vanilla, globe and lady's slipper orchids, and the enigmatic devil's claw. Butterflies abound, and you may see eagles, chamois and the Alpine marmot, too.

The closest Dolomite town to Venice, lying in the foothills of the mountains, is Belluno (➤ 175). This is a far cry from the German-speaking northern

Dolomites, but there is an Alpine air pervading. Close by is the Parco Naturale delle Dolomiti Bellunesi, an environmental project protecting the countryside and cultural heritage of the area. Tourists have been visiting since the 18th century, drawn by the spectacular scenery and Alpine plants and flowers. The park is actively promoting the continuation of the traditional environment by encouraging old farming methods and thus leaving the locality virtually unchanged. This is a fascinating region and a total contrast from the low-lying area of Venice and its islands.

To Belluno from Venezia San Lucia station By arranged tour, car or bus. Information from Venice tourist office or local travel agencies

LIDO DI JÉSOLO

This seaside resort is along the Adriatic coast 40km (25 miles) to the east of Venice and can be reached by bus from the city. Its sandy beach is 15km (9 miles) long and offers accommodation from hotels to villas and apartments to campsites. Although there has been a settlement here since Roman times, it only developed as a thriving resort after World War I and now more than 400,000 people visit every year. You can participate in all manner of activities: sailing, horse riding, go karting and, of course, swimming as well as enjoying a vibrant nightlife.

www.jesolo.it

🚤 The easiest way to get to Jésolo is by bus and then by boat. Ask at the tourist office

🛈 Piazza Brescia 13 ☎ 0421 370 601/602/603; also in summer at Piazza Torino ☎ 0421 363 607

PADOVA (PADUA)

The nearest large town to Venice, with a population of a quarter of a million, Padova can be reached by train, bus, car – or by boat. For the latter, the *Burchiello* and its rival the *Ville del Brenta*, sail between April and October from San Marco at about 9am (times and fares available from hotel concierges, travel agents and tourist information offices), cross the lagoon and cruise up the Brenta Canal, which is, in fact, a river. Stopping at several magnificent Renaissance villas on its banks and for lunch at a riverside restaurant, the boats arrive at Padua between 6 and 6.30pm and the 37km (23-mile) return journey to Venice is made by bus or train. A Venetian university city since the 15th century – and rich in buildings of that century – Padova is now dominated by commerce. **www.**turismopadova.it

🚌 53E 🚆 From Venezia San Lucia station

ℹ️ Galleria Pedrocchi ☎ 049 876 7927; Piazzale del Stazione ☎ 049 875 2077; Mar–Apr also Piazza del Santo ☎ 049 875 3087

POSSAGNO

Anyone eager to see more works of art should visit the village of Possagno, 72km (45 miles) northwest of Venice, the home of the sculptor Antonio Canova. Born here in 1757, Canova became the greatest of the neoclassical sculptors, producing smoothly graceful figures and delicate portraits, including his famous busts of Napoleon and Josephine, which are now in galleries throughout the world.

His house is now the centre of a gallery devoted to his works, mostly plaster models for statuary, and in the parish church which he gave to the village – the Tempio di Canova, inspired by the Parthenon in Athens and the Pantheon in Rome – is his tomb. However, only his body lies here; his heart remains in Venice, within the pyramid he himself designed for Titian in the great church of the Frari (► 50–51).

🚆 From Venezia San Lucia station to Bassano del Grappa then bus to Possagno (1 hour)

TREVISO

Treviso's walled centre is full of meandering old streets and brooding canals. The medieval and Renaissance buildings of Piazza dei Signori include the church of Santa Lucia, with frescoes by Tommaso da Modena (14th century). Gothic San Nicolò contains more da Modena frescoes on the columns as well as works by Lorenzo Lotto

and others, while the 15th- to 16th-century cathedral has a Titian altarpiece and an 11th-century baptistery. There is good Renaissance art in the Museo Civico.

www.provincia.treviso.it

🚌 8E 🚆 From Venezia San Lucia station

ℹ️ Piazzetta Monte di Pietà 8 ☎ 0422 547 632

TRIESTE

Much farther east of Venice than Lido di Jésolo is the great seaport of Trieste, once part of the Austro-Hungarian Empire and now connected to Venice by rail. A little farther to the north, just across the Slovenian border, is Lipica, where the Lipizzaner white horses are bred and can be ridden.

www.prolocotrieste.it

🚌 3, 6, 57, 66 🚆 From Venezia San Lucia station

ℹ️ Piazza Unità d'Italia 4B ☎ 040 347 8312

VERONA

Verona lies west of Vicenza (➤ opposite), close to Lake Garda and
some 98km (61 miles) from Venice. It is the second-biggest city
in the Veneto region after Venice. It is most famous as the setting
of Shakespeare's play *Romeo and Juliet* and for its Roman
remains, notably a magnificent arena, which is sometimes used
for performances of opera. Among Verona's other important
monuments is the unusually ornate Romanesque church of San
Zeno Maggiore (1123–35), with 11th–12th century bronze door
panels, a 'ship's keel' ceiling (1376) and an altarpiece by Mantegna
(1450s). The two main squares are the elegant Piazza dei Signori,
with the 12th-century Palazzo del Comune (town hall) among its
medieval and Renaissance civic gems, and the more workaday

Piazza delle Erbe, with a busy market. The powerful Scaligeri family, who governed the town from 1260 to 1387, are commemorated by a 14th-century bridge leading to the Castelvecchio (with an excellent art collection) and by the Arche Scaligere, their opulent tombs.

www.tourism.verona.it

🚊 From Venezia San Lucia station

ℹ️ Piazza Bra, Via degli Alpini 9 ☎ 045 806 8680

VICENZA

The capital of the Veneto is Vicenza, which lies 51km (32 miles) from Venice and is a handsome city, where the great architect Andrea di Palladio – a native of Padova – designed a dozen buildings.

Most famous of these is his eye-pleasingly symmetrical villa La Rotunda, which has been copied all over the world. Palladio's first public commission was the graceful double-colonnaded Basilica in Piazza dei Signori, where he also designed the Loggia del Capitaniato. Among the mass of other Palladio buildings are the Teatro Olimpico (1579), the oldest covered theatre in Europe, and many of the *palazzi* on Corso Andrea Palladio. The Museo Civico (in another Palladio building) has splendid Gothic and Renaissance art. Other older monuments include the Gothic churches of Santa Corona and San Lorenzo and some buildings on Contrà Porti, untouched by Palladio.

www.vicenza.org

🚊 From Venezia San Lucia station

ℹ️ Piazza Matteotti 12 ☎ 0444 320 854; also office at Piazza dei Signori 8
☎ 0444 544 122

Index

Street Index

187

Acknowledgements

The Automobile Association would like to thank the following photographers, companies and picture libraries for their assistance in the preparation of this book.

Abbreviations for the picture credits are as follows – (t) top; (b) bottom; (c) centre; (l) left; (r) right; (AA) AA World Travel Library.

6/7 Santa Maria della Salute AA/S Sawyer; **8/9** Gondolier AA/A Mockford & N Bonetti; **10bl** View from Campanile AA/A Mockford & N Bonetti; **10/11t** Santa Maria della Salute AA/C Sawyer; **10/11b** Molo and Palazzo Ducale from the Campanile AA/A Mockford & N Bonetti; **11cl** Basilica di San Marco AA/A Mockford & N Bonetti; **12bl** Rialto market AA/C Sawyer; **12br** Market AA/S McBride; **12/13t** Pescheria AA/S McBride; **12/13c** Squid AA/C Sawyer; **13cl** Seafood AA/C Sawyer; **14tl** Fruit and vegetables AA/R Walford; **14cl** Bakery AA/A Mockford & N Bonetti; **14/15t** Rialto fish market AA/A Mockford & N Bonetti; **14/15b** Café AA/D Miterdiri; **15tr** Scampi AA/A Mockford & N Bonetti; **15b** Caffe Florian AA/C Sawyer; **16bl** Piazza San Marco AA/S McBride; **16bc** Caffe Florian AA/A Mockford & N Bonetti; **16/17t** Grand Canal AA/C Sawyer; **17tr** Columns of San Marco AA/S McBride; **17br** Rialto bridge AA/A Mockford & N Bonetti; **18cl** Domes of the Basilica AA/S McBride; **18bl** Basilica di San Marco AA/A Mockford & N Bonetti; **18/19** San Giorgio Maggiore from the Campanile AA/S McBride; **19tr** Paolin ice-cream shop AA/R Walford; **19br** Grand Canal AA/R Newton; **20/21** Carnival AA/D Miterdiri; **24bl** Carnival AA/D Miterdiri; **26cr** Marco Polo airport AA/C Sawyer; **27tr** Vaporetto AA/A Mockford & N Bonetti; **27cl** Gondola AA/S McBride; **28** Water taxi AA/S McBride; **31br** Pharmacy sign AA/A Mockford & N Bonetti; **32tr** Carabinieri AA/A Mockford & N Bonetti; **34/35** Santa Maria della Salute AA/A Mockford & N Bonetti; **36/37** Piazza San Marco AA/A Mockford & N Bonetti; **37tr** Cupola AA/C Sawyer; **38/39** Palazzo on the Grand Canal AA/C Sawyer; **39tl** Palazzo Dario AA/C Sawyer; **40/41t** Bellini and Giorgione canvases AA/A Mockford & N Bonetti; **40/41b** Vivarini paintings AA/A Mockford & N Bonetti; **42b** Palazzo Ducale AA/A Mockford & N Bonetti; **42/43** Gothic tracery AA/A Mockford & N Bonetti; **44/45b** Piazza San Marco AA/A Mockford & N Bonetti; **45tl** Feeding pigeons AA/A Mockford & N Bonetti; **46/47** San Giorgio Maggiore AA/S McBride; **48/49b** Santi Giovanni e Paolo interior AA/S McBride; **48/49t** Exterior AA/S McBride; **49br** Tomb of Doge Michele Steno AA/R Newton; **50bl** Monument to Antonio Canova AA/C Sawyer; **50cr** Statue AA/S McBride; **50/51** Choir stalls AA/C Sawyer; **52b** Entrance detail AA/S McBride; **52/53t** Grand Canal and Santa Maria della Salute AA/S McBride; **54cl** San Rocco exterior AA/A Mockford & N Bonetti; **54/55** Interior AA/A Mockford & N Bonetti; **56/57** Grand Canal AA/A Mockford & N Bonetti; **58bl** Restaurant AA/A Mockford & N Bonetti; **60/61** View from San Giorgio Maggiore AA/S McBride; **62/63** Campo Santa Margherita AA/S McBride; **64/65** Santa Maria dei Miracoli AA/A Mockford & N Bonetti; **66** Masks AA/S McBride; **68b** Madonna and Child between Saints Nicholas, Peter, Mark and Benedict by Giovanni Bellini AA/C Sawyer; **70/71** Ferry AA/C Sawyer; **72b** Fondaco dei Turchi AA/A Mockford & N Bonetti; **74/75** Daniele hotel AA/D Miterdiri; **76/77** Fondamenta Zattere AA/S McBride; **79bl** Basilica di San Marco AA/S McBride; **80cl** Caffe Florian AA/A Mockford & N Bonetti; **80/81** Campanile di San Marco AA/A Mockford & N Bonetti; **82tr** Portrait of Doge Giovanni Mocenigo by Gentile Bellini AA/D Miterdiri; **83** Palazzo Contarini del Bovolo AA/A Mockford & N Bonetti; **84/85** The Education of the Virgin by Tiepolo AA/A Mockford & N Bonetti; **85br** San Moise AA/S McBride; **86** Street signs AA/C Sawyer; **87tr** La Fenice sign AA/C Sawyer; **88/89** San Salvador AA/A Mockford & N Bonetti; **90** Torre dell'Orologio AA/R Newton; **101** San Francesco della Vigna AA/D Miterdiri; **102/103** Canal near Campo Santa Maria Formosa AA/A Mockford & N Bonetti; **104cl** Ceremonial barge AA/C Sawyer; **104/105** Riva degli Schiavoni AA/S McBride; **106l** Giardini Pubblici AA/S McBride; **106/107** Castello district AA/S McBride; **108/109b** San Giovanni in Bragora AA/A Mockford & N Bonetti; **108tr** San Giorgio dei Greci AA/D Miterdiri; **109cr** Santa Maria Formosa AA/A Mockford & N Bonetti; **110/111b** Scuola Grande di San Marco AA/S McBride; **111tl** Statue, San Zaccaria AA/D Miterdiri; **112** Scuola di San Giorgio degli Schiavoni AA/D Miterdiri; **117b** Ca' d'Oro lion statues AA/A Mockford & N Bonetti; **118tl** Ca' d'Oro loggia shadows AA/A Mockford & N Bonetti; **118/119** Campo dei Mori AA/A Mockford & N Bonetti; **120tl** Madonna dell'Orto AA/S McBride; **121t** Sant'Alvise interior AA/A Mockford & N Bonetti; **122tl** San Geremia e Lucia AA/A Mockford & N Bonetti; **122/123b** Santa Maria dei Miracoli AA/A Mockford & N Bonetti; **124** Santa Maria di Nazaretta AA/A Mockford & N Bonetti; **129** San Stae AA/A Mockford & N Bonetti; **130/131** Campo San Polo AA/A Mockford & N Bonetti; **131t** Rialto fish market AA/A Mockford & N Bonetti; **132** On the Rialto Bridge AA/A Mockford & N Bonetti; **134/135** San Pantalon AA/S McBride; **141** Campo San Barnaba AA/S McBride; **142cl** Ca' Rezzonico AA/C Sawyer; **142/143** Campo San Barnaba AA/S McBride; **144tr** Gardens of the Peggy Guggenheim Collection AA/S McBride; **144cr** Dogana di Mare AA/D Miterdiri; **145** Peggy Guggenheim Collection AA/S McBride; **146/147t** La Giudecca island AA/S McBride; **146b** Gesuati AA/S McBride; **148bl** Campo Santa Margherita AA/A Mockford & N Bonetti; **148/149** Pulpit detail in Angelo Raffaele AA/A Mockford & N Bonetti; **150/151b** Accademia bridge AA/A Mockford & N Bonetti; **150/151tl** Il Redentore AA/A Mockford & N Bonetti; **151br** Santa Maria dei Carmini interior AA/A Mockford & N Bonetti; **152/153** Statue of Veronese, San Sebastiano AA/A Mockford & N Bonetti; **154tl** Squero di San Trovaso AA/D Miterdiri; **154** Zattere AA/S McBride; **159** Hungaria Palace Hotel, the Lido AA/A Mockford & N Bonetti; **160/161t** Burano AA/C Sawyer; **160/161b** Lace making AA/S McBride; **163b** Murano glass beads AA/A Mockford & N Bonetti; **164/165** San Michele AA/A Mockford & N Bonetti; **166** Basilica Santa Maria dell'Assunta, Torcello AA/A Mockford & N Bonetti; **168bl** Murano glass AA/C Sawyer; **168/169t** Lagoon AA/D Miterdiri; **172/173** Cortina d'Ampezzo, Belluno Fototeca ENIT; **174/175** Belluno Fototeca ENIT; **176tl** Monte Cristallo, Belluno Fototeca ENIT; **176/177b** Cortina d'Ampezzo, Belluno Fototeca ENIT; **178/179** Prato della Valle, Padova Fototeca ENIT; **180/181** Grounds of the Duomo, Treviso AA/C Sawyer; **181br** Piazza dell'Unita d'Italia, Trieste Fototeca ENIT; **182/183** Teatro Romano, Verona AA/A Mockford & N Bonetti; **183tr** Roman gate, Verona AA/A Mockford & N Bonetti.

Every effort has been made to trace the copyright holders, and we apologise in advance for any accidental errors. We would be happy to apply the corrections in the following edition of this publication.

Sight locator index

This index relates to the maps on the cover. We have given map references to the main sights in the book. Some sights may not be plotted on the maps.